Don T. Phillips

Dedication

Pastor Henry Sanders

Faith Outreach Christian Center

Navasota, Texas

He was there with me in

My darkest Hour......

Preface

Both the Old Testament and the New Testament of the Holy Scriptures contain references to the *Day of the Lord.* There are over 18 references to the Day of the Lord in the Old Testament and over 5 in the New Testament. There are also several places where the Day of the Lord is identified by a different term. The New Testament calls it a Day of Wrath, a Day of Visitation, and the Great Day of God Almighty. In all cases the Day of the Lord has yet to be fulfilled as a final and complete victory over Satan and sin. (Isaiah 22; Jeremiah 30:1-17; Joel 1-2; Amos 5; Zephaniah 1). The Day of the lord has frequently been identified as an extended period of time over which the Wrath of God is directed to an evil and unbelieving world, but we will show that this theology is incorrect and is based upon a lack of knowledge of how the Book of Revelation is structured. We will show that the Day of the Lord is exactly *a single day* which will come to pass in two different places.

Every mention of the Day of the Lord is consistent although sometimes obscure; It is a day of *darkness* and *gloom*; a day of *terror* and *wrath*; a day of *trouble* and *vengeance*; and a day of *waste* and *desolation*. The Day of the Lord is a certain time in which *God* will deal with wicked men directly and dramatically in fearful judgment destruction. A day is coming when God will punish sinful man here on earth, and He will deal with all unbelievers who are alive here on earth in wrath and in righteous indignation. The Day of the Lord is neither the *Bema Seat Judgment* nor the *Great White Throne Judgment*, but it is a "day" on which the Lord will punish all unbelievers here on earth.

One of the first Old Testament prophecies of the Day of the Lord is given by Zepeniah.

[15] *That day is a day of wrath, a day of trouble and distress, a day of wasteness and desolation, a day of darkness and gloominess, a day of clouds and thick darkness,*
[16] *A day of the trumpet and alarm against the fenced cities, and against the high towers.*
[17] *And I will bring distress upon men, that they shall walk like blind men, because they have sinned against the LORD: and their blood shall be poured out as dust, and their flesh as the dung.*
[18] *Neither their silver nor their gold shall be able to deliver them in the day of the LORD's wrath; but the whole land shall be devoured by the fire of his jealousy: for he shall make even a speedy riddance of all them that dwell in the land*   Zepeniah 15-18

The prophet Joel was one of the last Old Testament prophets to speak of the Day of the Lord.

[1] *Blow ye the trumpet in Zion, and sound an alarm in my holy mountain: let all the inhabitants of the land tremble: for the day of the LORD cometh, for it is nigh at hand;*
[2] *A day of darkness and of gloominess, a day of clouds and of thick darkness, as the morning spread upon the mountains: a great people and a strong; there hath not been ever the like, neither shall be any more after it, even to the years of many generations*   Joel 2: 1-2

An important prophecy which was key in determining when the Day of the Lord will occur is found in the Book of Acts.

The sun shall be turned into darkness, and the moon into blood, before that great and notable Day of the Lord come   Acts 2:20

It will be shown that there are two different Days of the Lord. (1) The *first* **Day of the Lord** is the final day of the Great Tribulation (The last day of Daniel's 70th Week). It will coincide with the 7th and last Bowl judgment of seven consecutive bowls and the *Battle of Armageddon.*

day to the *Battle of Armageddon* will be confirmed and justified by comparing key biblical prophecies with the Great Tribulation as seen by John in the Book of Revelation. However, it is difficult to associate the following prophecy by Peter with the Battle of Armageddon at the end of the Tribulation period.

[**10**] *But the day of the Lord will come as a thief in the night; in the which the heavens shall pass away with a great noise, and the elements shall melt with fervent heat, the earth also and the works that are therein shall be burned up.*
[**11**] *Seeing then that all these things shall be dissolved, what manner of persons ought ye to be in all holy conversation and godliness,*
[**12**] *Looking for and hasting unto the coming of the day of God, wherein the heavens being on fire shall be dissolved, and the elements shall melt with fervent heat?*
[**13**] *Nevertheless we, according to his promise, look for new heavens and a new earth, wherein dwelleth righteousness*   II Peter 3: 10-13

(2) It will be shown that this particular *Day of the Lord* which is prophesied by Peter is not referring to the Battle of Armageddon, but is referencing the last battle between Satan and God which will take place on a single day at the end of the 1000-year Millennial Kingdom. This is called *Satan's Last Stand* (Phillips, The Book of Revelation: *Mysteries Revealed*).

The Apostle Paul writes of another day which he uniquely calls the *Day of Jesus Christ.* There are several biblical verses in the New Testament which predict this day. It will be shown that this is prophesying of the *Rapture* which is described by the Apostle Paul and by Christ Himself.

Biblical scriptural investigation is clear that these three great events *will* take place, but not *when* they will take place. No one but God knows the exact day and year when these things will come to pass, but it is possible to suggest the time and seasons when all three will take place. Biblical Clues will be strengthened by comparing Jewish Messianic expectations with the prophetic structure of the *7 Feasts of Israel*. There are six Chapters in this book.

Chapter 1: Introduction

Chapter 1 will introduce and overview both the *Day of the Lord* and the *Day of Jesus Christ.* In order to frame both within the Book of Revelation, the 7 Seals, the 7 Trumpet Judgments and the 7 Bowls of God's Wrath are presented. Rapture of the saints, the Wrath of God and the Wrath of Satan are then defined and discussed.

Chapter 2: The *Day of the Lord*

Old Testament and New Testament scriptural references to the *Day of the Lord* are presented and discussed. It is shown that the Day of the Lord in the Old Testament is the *Battle of Armageddon.*

Chapter 3: The *Day of Jesus Christ*

The *Day of Jesus Christ* is a term unique to the Apostle Paul. It can be shown that the Day of Jesus Christ is the day when Christ returns in the air to Resurrect and Rapture the saints. When the epistle of II Peter is carefully studied and contrasted to Old Testament references to the Day of the Lord, several inconsistencies and differences are evident. This leads to a conjecture that Paul is not describing either the Battle of Armageddon or the Rapture, but a final day of battle between God himself and Satan. This is called *Satan's Last Stand* and it will end the 1000-Year Millennial Kingdom.

The conclusion is that the traditional Old Testament *Day of the Lord* and the New Testament *Day of Jesus Christ* are separate terms for two separate events. In addition, the Apostle Peter in his epistle *II Peter* was writing to new converts from the Jews first, and then the Gentiles. In II Peter 3: 1-10, Peter uses the term Day of the Lord to refer to the final battle with Satan and his unbelievers at the end of the 1000-year Millennial Kingdom. This final battle is fought by God Himself.

Authors Comment: The 12 disciples (including Matthias) were anointed by God to spread the gospel message of salvation by faith first to the Jews and then to the Gentiles. Conversely, only the Apostle Paul was chosen to take the New Covenant to the Gentiles first, and then to the Jews. Hence, the Jewish converts were confused: Should they completely abandon all the Covenant promises made to the Jews? This would include the promise that God had made to Abraham, Moses and King David that the Jews were promised that they would dwell and prosper in the Land of Canaan.

God cannot fail to honor His unconditional promises. The purpose of the 1000-year Millennial Kingdom was to finally fulfill this promise. The Jews would live in the promised land for 1000 year. After the 1000 years have been fulfilled, the Jews who accepted Jesus Christ as their Lord and Savior would inherit t Kingdom of God which is restoration of men (no sin) and the land (no curse) forever, and the world would be restored to an Edenic state. II Peter Chapter 3 assures all Jews that one day all evil would be purged from the land and that the land would also be purified. Evil and sin will not inherit eternity just as Sodom and Gomorrah and the people of Noah's day all destroyed. Paul then evidently spoke of this day in II Peter 3: 8-13.

Chapter 4: The Seven Seals

All Pre-Rapture, Mid-Tribulation and classic Pre-Wrath Rapture theories have a fatal flaw in how they depict the chronological sequencing of the 7 Seals, the 7-Trumpet Judgments and the 7 Bowl Judgments. Chapter 4 will prove from the Book of Revelation that the Seals-Trumpets-Bowls cannot be linked in a serial execution. The Seals only provide an overview of conditions and specific events that will occur over the Tribulation Period.

Chapter 5: Rapture of the Saints

The Rapture of the Saints is almost totally an event which is revealed by the Apostle Paul (I Thessalonians 4: 13-18, I Corinthians 15: 50-53, II Corinthians 12: 1-6). Paul was chosen By Jesus Christ after His death to reveal the *mystery* of the New Covenant to Jews and Gentiles alike. The Rapture was previously spoken of by Jesus Christ (Matthew 24: 29-31) as He prepared His 12 disciples for His departure and sacrificial death. The Rapture is such an important issue to most Christians that an entire Chapter is devoted to its explanation. Chapter 5 will summarize the four most common theories concerning the Rapture, and then a *new Pre-Wrath Rapture* theory will be presented and supported by scripture which resolves all problems.

Chapter 6: Parables and the Tribulation Timeline

The key to understanding the timing of the Day of Christ to the Day of the Lord can be found in an unlikely place: In the Parables of the *Soil and the Sower* and the Parable of the *Wheat and Tares*. These two Parables were spoken to His disciples by Jesus Christ, and they contain the key to properly linking and sequencing the Day of the Lord (The Battle of Armageddon) and the Day of Jesus Christ (The Rapture of the saints). This Chapter will link these two parables to the Book of Revelation and show that they parallel these two events.

Chapter 7: *Mysteries* Resolved

Chapter 6 will summarize what is meant by the *Day of the Lord* (Two different occasions) and the *Day of Jesus Christ*. Each will be defined and summarized with scriptural support. The Mystery of when these two events (relative time and season) will take place will be determined and supported by the Holy Scriptures and the words of Jesus Christ in the *Olivet Discourse.*

This book is not long, but has a large number of important conclusions…. all justified by the Holy Scriptures. Even though it is relatively short, it cannot be read casually but requires an investigation of a large number of Old Testament and New Testament biblical verses. Open your mind and prove everything by the Word of God.

Dr. Don T. Phillips

July, 2023

Table of Contents

Chapter 1

Introduction

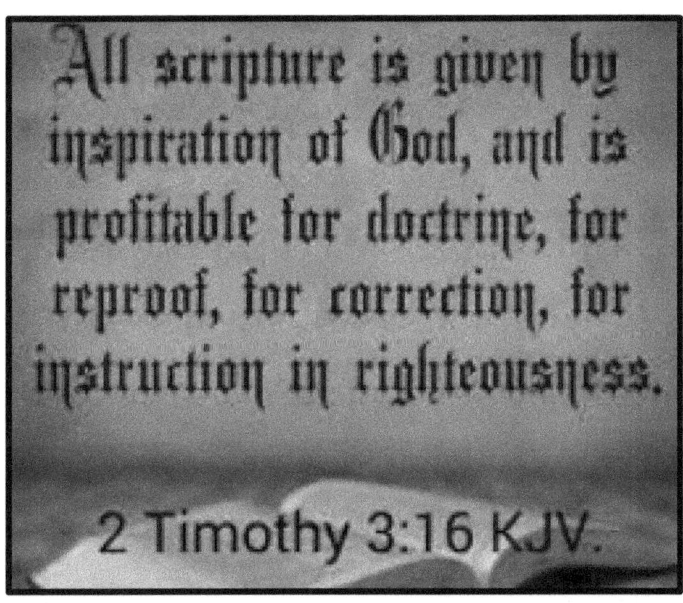

Paul wrote 13 epistles (letters) to individuals and churches which he had founded in Asia (Asia Minor). The second Epistle written to Timothy is generally regarded as the last that was written by Paul. Tradition holds that he was beheaded in Rome and died as a martyr for his faith. The epistle of II Timothy is different from the other books that Paul wrote. He completely and authoritatively had revealed the New Covenant of faith and grace in his previous letters, and now he was ready to die. He repeatedly admonished all Christians to be ready and equipped to present the Gospel message to all unbelievers, and He addressed how every Christian should live under the New Covenant.

In the 13 letters which Paul wrote he made reference to a particular future time called the *Day of the Lord* (I Corinthians 1:8, I Corinthians 5:5, II Corinthians 1:14, I Thessalonians 5:2). The Holy Scriptures refer to this same time in a variety of ways. The expression Day of Lord is synonymous with the *Day of Visitation* (I Peter 2:12), the *Day of Lord*

Jesus (II Corinthians 1:14), the *Day of Judgment* (I John 4:17), the *Great and Awesome Day* (Joel 2:31), the *Day of Vengeance* (Isaiah 61:2) and the *Great Day of God Almighty* (Revelation 16:14). Other passages refer to this same time as simply *The Day, That Day* or the *Day of God.*

Several Old Testament writers while under the inspiration of the Holy Spirit had announced the coming Day of the Lord (Isaiah 2:2-4; Isaiah 13:6-13, 9; Ezekiel 30:3; Joel 1:15; Joel 2:1, Joel 2:11, Joel 2:31; Obadiah 1:15; Zephaniah 1:7-8, 14; Zechariah 14:1).

Considering the frequent reference to the Day of the Lord in both the Old and New Testaments, most Christians never take the time or effort to understand what these terms stand for or what role they play in the eternal plan of God. We will see that these terms which reference the Day of the Lord are not all describing the same event. This will be clear as this book is studied.

Day of the Lord: *Overview*

The first reference to this Day in the holy scriptures (KJV) appears to be in Isaiah 2:12.

*For the **Day of the LORD** of hosts shall be upon every one that is proud and lofty, and upon every one that is lifted up; and he shall be brought low*   Isaiah 2:12   As the Old Testament is read and studied, the Day of the Lord is referred to more than two dozen times. It most commonly appears in the books of Isaiah, Joel, Jeremiah and Zephaniah. As we have shown, references to this Day can be found in both the major and minor prophets, Lamentations and even the Plasms of David. The Day of the Lord is a day filled with dichotomies. For some, it represents a day of terror, for others a day of vengeance. For all Christians, we will see that this day should be one of victory, while for all unbelievers it is a day of defeat and victory over sin. Ultimately, it is a day of retribution and victory over Satan and sinful unbelievers. Jesus Christ spoke of this day and prophesied that it will be a day of rejoicing for some and a day of sorrow for others (Matthew 24:50, Luke 12:46). As we unravel the *Mystery* of this day it will be discovered and scripturally justified that the Holy Scriptures are actually speaking of two different days.

Zephaniah reveals to us that the *Day of the Lord* is a day of trouble. It will be a day of darkness, and desolation.

[14] *The great **Day of the LORD** is near, it is near, and hastens greatly, even the voice of the day of the LORD: the mighty man shall cry there bitterly.*
[15] *That day is a day of wrath, a day of trouble and distress, a day of wasteness and desolation, a day of darkness and gloominess, a day of clouds and thick darkness*   Zepeniah 1: 14-15

The prophet Joel also has a great deal to say about the *Day of the Lord.*

[15] *The sun and the moon shall be darkened, and the stars shall withdraw their shining.*
[16] *The LORD also shall roar out of Zion, and utter his voice from Jerusalem; and the heavens and the earth shall shake: but the LORD will be the hope of his people, and the strength of the children of Israel.*
[17] *So shall ye know that I am the LORD your God dwelling in Zion, my holy mountain: then shall Jerusalem be holy, and there shall no strangers pass through her any more*   Joel 3:15-17

Joel prophesies that there will be multitudes gathered to conquer God's people and the holy City of Jerusalem in a place called the *valley of decision* where a great battle will take place (Joel 3: 7-13). This conflict between God and the Nations that seek to destroy Israel will take place in the *Valley of Jehosephat.* Biblical scholars and archeologists have identified this valley as a large, fertile plain just north of Jerusalem. It is widely believed that this is where the great *Battle of Armageddon* will take place when Christ returns as a conquering King. All unbelievers will be summoned to this Valley in a military campaign which we will call the *Jerusalem Campaign.* All but a few unbelievers will be assembled to attack Jerusalem and the Jews (Matthew 25: 31-46).

Just as Satan is about to attack Jerusalem to destroy all Christians and Jews in the City, Jesus Christ will descend from heaven to engage Satan and his forces. He will descend to the Mount of Olives and His feet will straddle the mountain, splitting it into two parts.

[1] *Behold, the day of the LORD cometh, and thy spoil shall be divided in the midst of thee.*
[2] *For I will gather all nations against Jerusalem to battle; and the city shall be taken, and the houses rifled, and the women ravished; and half of the city shall go forth into captivity, and the residue of the people shall not be cut off from the city.*
[3] *Then shall the LORD go forth, and fight against those nations, as when he fought in the day of battle.*
[4] *And his feet shall stand in that day upon the mount of Olives, which is before Jerusalem on the east, and the mount of Olives shall cleave in the midst thereof toward the east and toward the west, and there shall be a very great valley; and half of the mountain shall remove toward the north, and half of it toward the south*   Zachariah 14: 1-4

The *Battle of Armageddon* will take place that same day on the last day of the Church Age. It is vividly described by the prophet John in the Book of Revelation.

[11] *And I saw heaven opened, and behold a white horse; and he that sat upon him was called Faithful and True, and in righteousness he doth judge and make war.*
[12] *His eyes were as a flame of fire, and on his head were many crowns; and he had a name written, that no man knew, but he himself.*
[13] *And he was clothed with a vesture dipped in blood: and his name is called The Word of God.*
[14] *And the armies which were in heaven followed him upon white horses, clothed in fine linen, white and clean.*
[15] *And out of his mouth goeth a sharp sword, that with it he should smite the nations: and he shall rule them with a rod of iron: and he treads the winepress of the fierceness and wrath of Almighty God.*

[**16**] *And he hath on his vesture and on his thigh a name written, KING OF KINGS, AND LORD OF LORDS.* Revelation 19: 11-16

In Chapter 2, it will be shown beyond any reasonable doubt that the Battle of Armageddon is the prophesied *Day of the Lord* when Christ will return to earth in His 2nd advent as a conquering King. The Battle of Armageddon will be swift and decisive.

The Day of Christ: *Overview*

Often associated (wrongly) with the Day of the Lord is the *Day of Christ.* It is also called the *Day of the Lord Jesus* (I Corinthians 5:5, II Corinthians 1:14). The *Day of Christ* is a phrase unique to the writings of Paul (Philippians 1:6, Philippians 1:10, 10, Philippians 2:16, I Corinthians 1:8).

Being confident of this very thing, that he which hath begun a good work in you will perform it until the **Day of Jesus Christ** Philippians 1:6

That ye may approve things that are excellent; that ye may be sincere and without offence till the **Day of Christ** Philippians 1:10

As also ye have acknowledged us in part, that we are your rejoicing, even as ye also are ours in the **Day of the Lord Jesus**
II Corinthians 1:14

[**20**] *For our conversation is in heaven; from whence also we look for the Savior, the Lord Jesus Christ:*
[**21**] *Who shall change our vile body, that it may be fashioned like unto his glorious body, according to the working whereby he is able even to subdue all things unto himself* Philippians 3: 20-21

It will be shown in Chapter 2 that the *Day of Jesus Christ* corresponds to the *Rapture* described by both the apostle Paul (I Thessalonians 4: 15-17, Philippians 3: 20-21, I Corinthians 51-53) and by Christ Himself

(Matthew 24: 30-31). The *Day of the Lord* corresponds to the Great *Battle of Armageddon* (Isaiah 13: 4-13).

Chronology and Sequencing of the Great Tribulation
In order to accurately and correctly place both the Day of the Lord (Battle of Armageddon) and the Day of Jesus Christ (Rapture), it is necessary to understand *when* these two events will take place. This can be determined from the Book of Revelation.

The order in which the Book of Revelation is written and a summary of conditions/events which transpire are shown on the next page. The Apostle John is called to heaven by God to reveal what will happen in the latter days. Seven is God's perfect number, and there are three sequences of 7 which are revealed in the Book of Revelation (Seals-Bowls and Trumpets). These 7 sequences of events are preceded by an interlude of Revelation 1-5.

Interlude:
   Chapter 1 …... John has been exiled to the Island of Patmos as an enemy of the Roman Empire. he is living in a cave, and suddenly God visits him. God appears to John in all of His heavenly glory and instructs him:

> *Write the things which thou hast seen, and the things which are, and the things which shall be hereafter*   Revelation 1:19

   Chapter 2 and 3…...The 1st thing that God instructs John to do is to write 7 letters to each of the 7 churches in Asia (Asia Minor). Each letter contains a commendation and possible condemnation of each church for its activities.

The Church in **Ephesus**………. The **Apostolic** Churc h

The Church in **Smyrma**………. The *Persecuted* Church

The Church in **Pergamos**……… The *Tolerant* Church

The Church in **Thyatira**…………The *Apostate* Church

The Church in **Sardis**……………The *Dead* Church

The Church in **Philadelphia**……. The *Faithful* Church

The Church in **Laodicea**………   The *Lifeless* Church

(For a detailed study of the 7 Churches see Phillips, The Book of Revelation: *Mysteries Revealed*.)

Chapter 4………The apostle John is told to come up here (Revelation 4:1). He ascends to heaven *in the spirit* and he sees the throne of God surrounded by *four wild beasts* and *24 elders*.

Chapter 5……… John sees God the Father siting upon his throne of glory and He has a large scroll in his right hand. The scroll is sealed with seven seals. John clearly sees all 7 seals and this is proof that the content of the scroll cannot be read until all 7 seals have been removed (broken).

Note: An important event which will be subsequently discussed in some detail is called the *Rapture*. An overwhelming number of modern preachers and biblical *scholars* will teach that when John is called to heaven from the Island of Patmos, this represents the Rapture of the saints (alive and dead). Clearly, this precedes every event which will take place in the Great Period of Tribulation. This is called a *Pretribulation Rapture* because it is obvious that it takes place before any of the seals are removed, and the contents of this scroll contain what will happen during the Tribulation. A Pretribulation rapture will be shortly discussed in some detail.

The Lord is holding the large scroll with 7 seals, and suddenly John hears a mighty angel proclaim: *Who is worthy to open the book, and to loosen the seals?* No one was able to answer, and John began weeping bitterly because there was no one who could break or remove the 7 seals. As John stood weeping, one of the 24 elders stood up and said: *Weep not: behold, the Lion of the tribe of Juda, the Root of David, hath prevailed to open the book, and loose the seven seals thereof* (Revelation 5:5). John then sees a

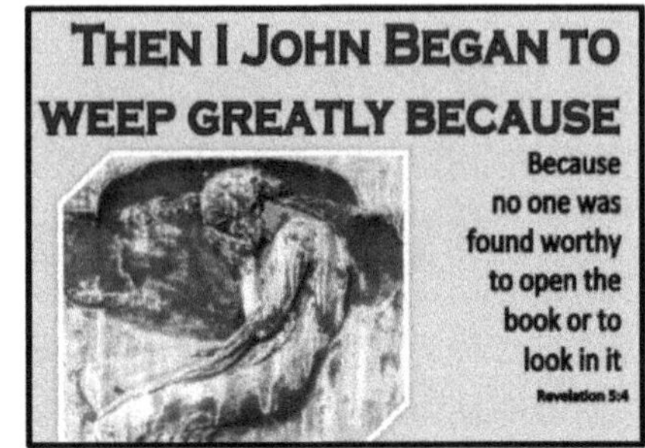

Lamb as if it had been slain standing among the 24 elders, and this lamb comes and takes the scroll from the right hand of God. What a powerful scene! The Lamb of God (Jesus Christ) is the only man in heaven, below heaven or above heaven who is worthy to reveal what will happen at the end of the Church age.

[**12**] *Saying with a loud voice, Worthy is the Lamb that was slain to receive power, and riches, and wisdom, and strength, and honor, and glory, and blessing.*
[**13**] *And every creature which is in heaven, and on the earth, and under the earth, and such as are in the sea, and all that are in them, heard I saying, Blessing, and honor, and glory, and power, be unto him that sits upon the throne, and unto the Lamb for ever and ever.*
Revelation 5:13

Jesus Christ is now authorized to open the 7 sealed scroll and reveal the fate of all mankind and the world which He has created. In Revelation 1:19, God told John on the Island of Patmos:

Write the things which thou hast seen (Revelation Chapter 1).
The things which are (Revelation Chapters 2-5.
The things which shall be hereafter (Revelation Chapters 6-22).

John is told to *come and see* (Revelation 6:1).

The Seven Seals, Seven Trumpets and Seven Bowls

Jesus Christ now begins to open the seven seals (Revelation 6:1). The overwhelming majority of seminary professors, preachers and biblical scholars assume that the Great Tribulation is initiated by the seven seals being broken/removed by Jesus Christ, and that each seal causes an event to occur which is lock-step sequenced with the 7 Trumpet Judgments (Revelation 8:6) and the 7 Bowl judgements (Revelation 16:1). Together these 21 events constitute what we call *The Great Tribulation*.

NUMBER	SEALS Opened by the Lamb	TRUMPETS Blown by seven angels	BOWLS Poured by seven angels
1.	White horse: conqueror	Hail and fire; 1/3 of vegetation burnt	Sores
2.	Red horse: war	Mountain of fire; 1/3 of creatures in sea destroyed	Sea becomes blood; all marine life dies
3.	Black horse: famine	Star called wormwood falls; 1/3 of fresh water poisoned	Fresh water turned to blood
4.	Pale horse: death	Partial darkness; 1/3 of sun, moon, and stars	Scorching sun burns men
5.	Martyrs reassured	Woe #1: Angel releases locusts from abyss	Darkness on beast's kingdom
6.	Great day of wrath: earthquake, signs in heaven	Woe #2: Four angels loosed at Euphrates; they slay 1/3 of earth's population	Euphrates dries up; kings assemble for war at Armageddon
7.	1/2 hour of silence: introduction of trumpets	Announcement of the Lord's victory	Severe earthquake and great hail

As Jesus Christ removes each seal, John is given a vision of things which are about to happen (Revelation 6:1). The Seals, Trumpets and Bowls are usually believed to span a period of 7. One way to connect the series of 21 events is to visualize Jesus Christ opening each of the 1st six seals and when the 7th seal is broken there are 30 minutes of complete silence in heaven (Revelation 8:1). At the end of 30 minutes, Christ begins to *unroll* the scroll and reveal its contents to John in a series of visions. Following the opening of the 6th seal, 7 angels come forth each carrying a trumpet. One by one the angels blow a trumpet, and each trumpet *launches* a corresponding event. When the 7th trumpet is blown, the earth is shaken (earthquakes), heavenly disturbances and hail falls upon the earth (Revelation 11:19). At that point in time a monumental cry is heard in heaven.

The kingdoms of this world are become the kingdoms of our Lord, and of his Christ; and he shall reign for ever and ever   Revelation 11:15

The prophetic message is clear and unmistakable: The time has come for Jesus Christ to assume his rightful position as King of Kings and Lord of Lords. However, the context demands that this is not immediate because there are still 7 angels who will come forth and pour out or unleash the 7 bowls. When the 7th bowl is poured out upon the earth, a great voice is heard from heaven which announces: *It is done!* (Revelation 16:18). After the 7th bowl is emptied, Christ will immediately return to fight Satan and his army of unbelievers at the Battle of Armageddon. This great battle will end the Church Age.   Following the Battle of Armageddon, the *Bema Seat Judgment* for rewards of all true believers (Jews and Gentiles) will take place, Christ will Judge the Nations at the *Sheep and Goats Judgment*, the Wedding Supper of the Lamb will be held and the 1000-year *Millennial Kingdom* will begin. A complete treatment of theses end-time events is beyond the scope of this book. The reader is referred to Phillips; The Book of Revelation: *Mysteries Revealed.*

John writes that he actually *saw* these thinks take place. Whether he saw these things in a series of prophetic visions, or whether he was actually transported in the spirit to those points in time and actually saw them take place in the spirit is not revealed, but we can be sure that they will soon take place and come to pass. It is also true that except for when the 7th Seal is removed (revelation 8:1) and the events of the 5th trumpet (Revelation 9:5), the time duration is not given in the Holy Scriptures. The Book of Revelation omits two significant details: (1) Since the time duration nor the starting-ending points for each seal, trumpet, and bowl except for two are not revealed: *How long will each event last? When will each start?* The duration of each event (Seal, Trumpet or Bowl) is completely unknown but it is certain that they are not of equal duration. All that is known is that once the 1st Trumpet is blown, they will all occur in lock-step sequence (2) A related question not independent of the previous question is: *How long will the Tribulation period last?*

The answer to this question can be found in the *Book of Daniel* (Daniel 9: 24-27) in the well-known *70-Week Prophecy* given to the prophet of Daniel while in Babylonian captivity. This prophecy is in response to Daniel asking the Lord to show him what would become of the Nation of Israel and the Jews. The Lord revealed that both would be preserved by God after 70 prophetic weeks of 490 years had come to pass. The final destiny of the Jews would be when the Church Age is completed over 2500 years into the future. Understanding and interpreting this prophecy has spawned hundreds of technical papers and many books. Unraveling the 70-Week Prophecy of Daniel is very difficult and requires several key assumptions which might be made.

This is far beyond the scope of this book, but the interested reader is referred to: Phillips; *The Daniel 70-Week Prophecy*. It is only important to note that depending upon when the Daniel prophecy began, the length of each prophetic week, and a number of other assumptions which must be made…. one can calculate that the Tribulation will last either 7 years or 3.5 years. We will shortly discuss Dniel's 70th Week and how it affects the *Day of the Lord* will shortly be discussed.

Rapture of the Saints

It is critical as we examine and interpret the *Day of the Lord* that an event called the *Rapture* is clearly understood. The Rapture of all true believers, living and dead, was a *mystery* that was explained and revealed by the apostle Paul.

[**51**] *Behold, I shew you a **mystery**; We shall not all sleep, but we shall all be changed,*
[**52**] *In a moment, in the twinkling of an eye, at the last trump: for the trumpet shall sound, and the dead shall be raised incorruptible, and we shall be changed.*
[**53**] *For this corruptible must put on incorruption, and this mortal must put on immortality.*   I Corinthians 15: 51-53

A mystery in the Bible is something that has either not been previously understood or previously disclosed. Paul revealed additional information about the Rapture to the saints in his letter to the Church at Thessalonica.

[**13**] *But I would not have you to be ignorant, brethren, concerning them which are asleep, that ye sorrow not, even as others which have no hope.*
[**14**] *For if we believe that Jesus died and rose again, even so them also which sleep in Jesus will God bring with him.*
[**15**] *For this we say unto you by the word of the Lord, that we which are alive and remain unto the coming of the Lord shall not prevent them which are asleep.*
[**16**] *For the Lord himself shall descend from heaven with a shout, with the voice of the archangel, and with the trump of God: and the dead in Christ shall rise first:*
[**17**] *Then we which are alive and remain shall be caught up together with them in the clouds, to meet the Lord in the air: and so shall we ever be with the Lord*   I Thessalonians 4: 13-17

There are several key things which Paul revealed concerning the Rapture.

(1)   The Rapture will occur suddenly and unexpectedly
(2)   It will occur at the *Last Trump*
(3)   Christ will not set his feet upon the earth, but He will meet all believers *in the air*
(4)   The *dead* in Christ will rise *first* to meet Christ and they will be *followed* by all believers who are *alive* and remain
(5)   Christ will descend from heaven with a *shout* and by the *voice* of an archangel (Probably Gabriel or Michael)
(6)   All who join Christ in the air will be given a new *incorruptible* and *immortal* body
(7)   The *Rapture* will only involve all *believers*…. living or dead.

The predominate belief among all modern prophecy teachers, students, and biblical scholars is that the Tribulation is 7 years in duration. The Rapture is not a subject of debate as to whether or not it *will occur*, but *when it will occur*. The following simplified diagrams illustrate a Pretribulation, Mid-tribulation, and Post-tribulation rapture.

A Typical 490 Year Daniel Prophecy with a Prophetic Gap and A 7-Year Tribulation

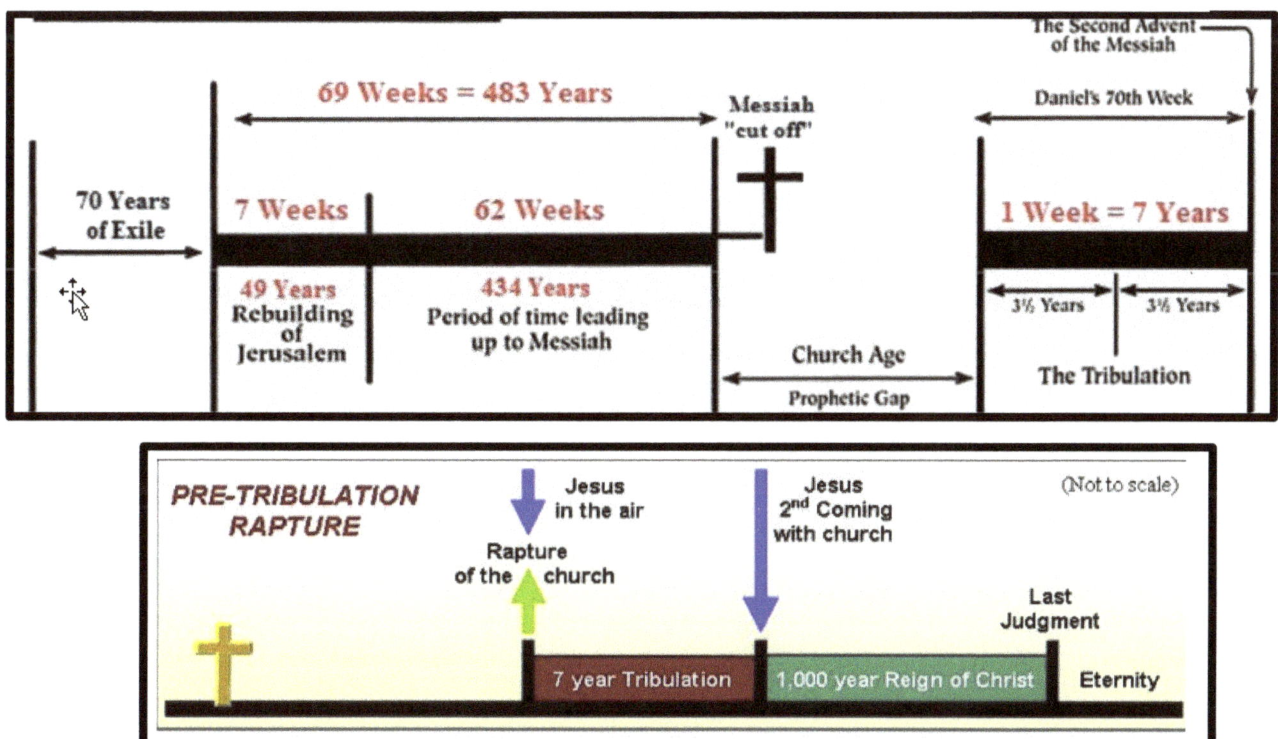

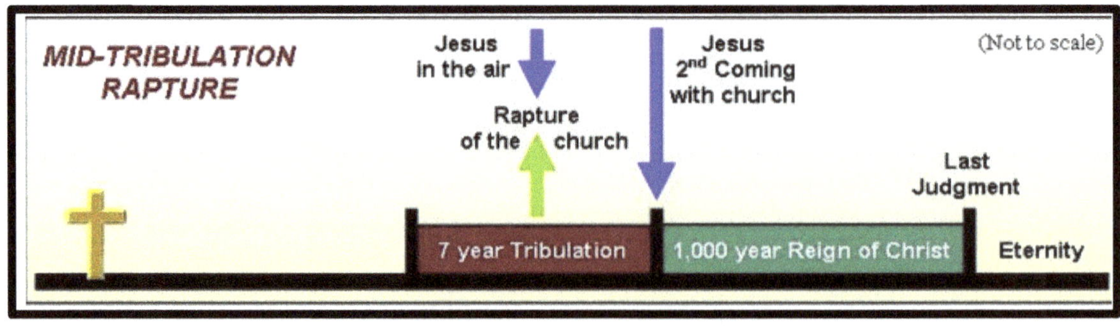

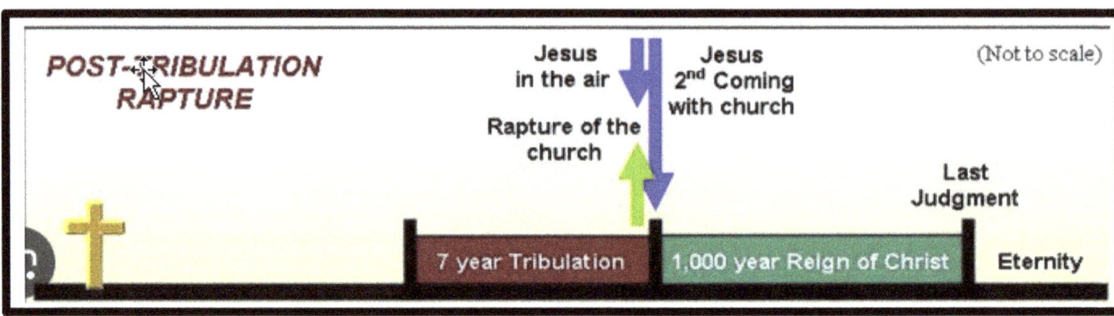

All three Rapture beliefs are exactly as they would seem, and all assume a 7-year Tribulation. The *Pre-Tribulation Rapture* places the Rapture before the Tribulation begins. The *Mid-Tribulation Rapture* assumes that the Rapture will occur after 3.5 years have elapsed. In both beliefs, the 1st seal begins the 7-year Tribulation, and most if not all are opened over the first 3.5 years. The *Post-Tribulation Rapture* assumes that the Rapture of all true believers take place just before the Battle of Armageddon, and then immediately return with Jesus Christ to fight the Battle of Armageddon. It is interesting, but all 7-year, Mid-Trib and Post-Trib Rapture's, require that Christians must go through 3.5 years of tribulation. In the classic Pre-tribulation belief, all Christians are raptured out just before the 1st Seal is removed. More to say about this later.

A more recent Rapture theory has been proposed by Van Kampen and Matthew Rosenthral. It assumes a 7-year Tribulation and is shown as follows.

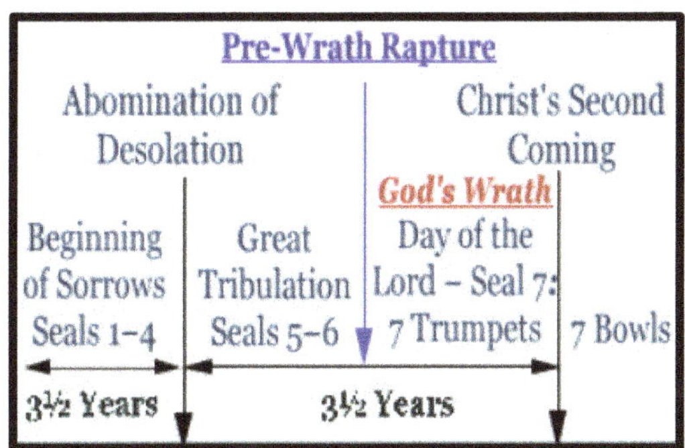

This *Pre-Wrath Rapture* theory will be discussed in more detail in Chapter 3, but for now note that the Rapture is proposed to occur *after* the 6th seal is broken, and before the 7th Seal is removed. *Why did Rosenthal and Van Kampen choose this location for the Rapture?* Their reasoning is based upon Revelation 6:17. The 6th Seal has been removed by Christ and John writes:

*For the **great day of his wrath is come**; and who shall be able to stand?* Revelation 6:17

Rosenthal and van Kampen both believed that: (1) The Rapture will occur when the 6th Seal is broken (2) The *Great Tribulation* would last 7 years (3) The 7 Seals, 7 Trumpets and 7 Bowls all occur in sequence (4) All born-again Christians are *not* destined to go through the *Wrath of God*. Since the ***great day of His wrath*** has arrived when the 6th seal is removed, this necessitates two critical conclusions: (1) There is no difference in the *Wrath of Satan* and the *Wrath of God*. The Wrath of Satan (the 7 Trumpet Judgments) and the Wrath of God (the 7 Bowl Judgments) are both just *Wrath* in Revelation 6:17 and (2) The *Great Day of His Wrath* (Revelation 6:17) cannot just a *single day* but at least 3.5 years (The reign of Antichrist and Satan). We will show that both of these two conclusions are incorrect in Chapters 2-4.

Since *God's Wrath* is clearly stated to have *come* in Revelation 6:17 after the 6th Seal has been removed, both Rosenthal and Van Kampen reasoned that all Christians would need to be raptured out *before* the 7 Trumpets (Wrath of Satan…Revelation 12:12) were blown and the 7 Bowls (Wrath of God…. Revelation 15:1, Revelation 16:1) were poured out upon the earth. The only question (in their minds) was: *During the 7-year Tribulation, when was the 6th Seal removed?* Both agreed that the Tribulation will begin as the 1st seal of the 6 sealed scroll is broken (removed), and that the first 3 seals are removed over the first half of a 7-year Tribulation. They called the first 3 seals *birth pains* (deception, wars and famines). Almost all scholars agree that the period of Great Tribulation will not begin until Satan is cast out of the heavenly realm by Michael and the Holy angels of God (Revelation 12: 1-10).

In either a Pre-Tribulation Rapture, a Mid-Tribulation Rapture, a Post-Tribulation Rapture, or a classic Pre-Wrath rapture……Satan cannot arise and persecute mankind until after 3.5 years have elapsed (Revelation 11:3, Revelation 12:14). Satan will be furious and attack all who remain upon the earth (Revelation 12:12). Satan will begin His deadly assault preceded by worldwide deception (Seal 1), War (Seal 2 and worldwide famine (Seal 3). When the 4th seal is removed, Power is given to Satan and his evil forces by God to kill ¼ of all mankind (there ae 8 billion people worldwide as of June, 2023). When Christ removes Seal 5, John sees a large number of blood-bought saints who have all been martyred for their faith in Christ crying out for vengeance. When Seal 6 is removed, several devastating and supernatural signs are seen by John: (1) The Sun becomes black (2) The moon turns to blood (3) The heavens depart as a scroll and (4) every mountain and island move out of their places. *Why are all these signs given when the 6th Seal is removed and the large scroll is still sealed and cannot be read?* This question will be investigated and answered in Chapters 3-4. Try to answer it now for you own understanding. Why are these things happening *before* any Trumpet has been blown and not one *Bowl of God's Wrath* has been poured out upon the earth? (Revelation 16:1 and Revelation 17 :1).

> ***Authors Comment***: Note that this puzzling question is not just applicable to a Mid-Tribulation or a Pre-Wrath theology, but applies to a Pre-Tribulation Rapture belief also. All Pre-tribulation Rapture theories believe that the Rapture will occur before the 1st Seal is removed: So, in fact, all

Pretribulation Rapture believers are also Pre -Wrath Rapture believers!!

When the 7th Seal is removed by Christ, there 30 minutes of silence in Heaven which are in anticipation of the 7 Trumpets which are about to sound.

The Wrath of Satan and the Wrath of God

The 7 Trumpets are called the *Wrath of Satan* (Revelation 12:12). The 7 Bowls are without a doubt the *Wrath of God* (Revelation 15:1, Revelation 15:7), Revelation 16:1).

The Holy Scriptures are quite clear that the Body of Christ is expected to experience Great Tribulation but no living Saint will ever experience the *Wrath of God.*

For the Wrath of God is revealed from heaven against all ungodliness and unrighteousness of men, who hold the truth in unrighteousness Romans 1:18

Much more then, being now justified by his blood, we shall be saved from wrath through him.   Romans 5:9

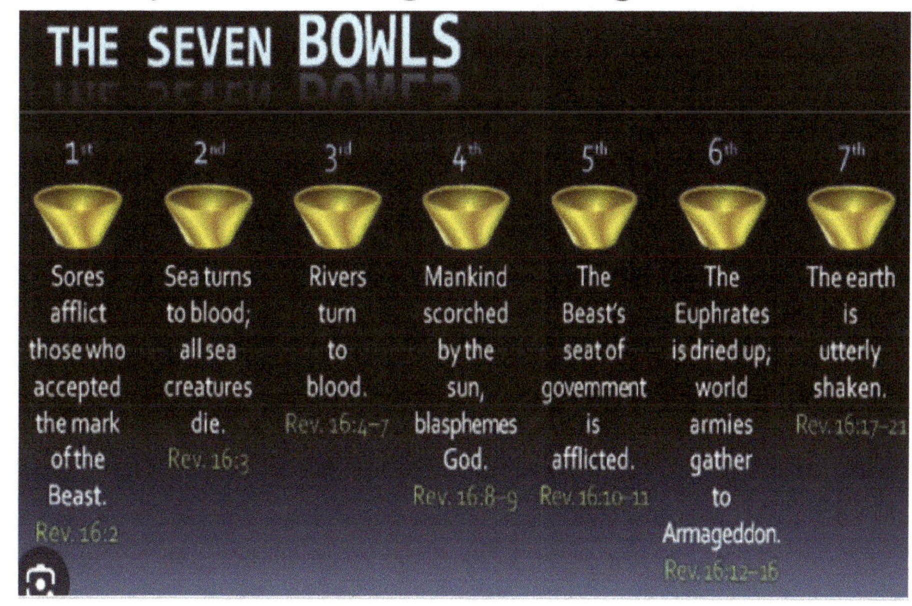

Let no man deceive you with vain words: for because of these things cometh the Wrath of God upon the children of disobedience
Ephesians 5:6

And to wait for his Son from heaven, whom he raised from the dead, even Jesus, which delivered us from the wrath to come.
I Thessalonians 1:10

As soon as the 7th Trumpet is blown it is announced that: *...the **mystery** of God should be finished, as he hath declared to his servants the prophets* (Revelation 10:7). What *mystery*? The Mystery of the New Covenant which is now freely offered to both Jews and Gentiles by *faith*. This is a clue that the 7-year tribulation will be over for all Born-Again Christians (John 3:3) when the 7th Trumpet sounds, since all Born-Again Christians are *promised* that they would never go through the Wrath of God.

The Pre-Wrath theory of Rosenthal and Van Kampen should be commended because it required some new out-of-the-box thinking. However, it is full of inconsistencies and erroneous conclusions. Chapters 3 and 4 will present a new Pre-Rapture Theory which will resolve all difficulties and is biblically consistent. It is now time to discuss the *Day of the Lord.*

Chapter 2

The Day of the Lord

The Holy Scriptures are full of mysterious and clouded references to what is called the *Day of the Lord*. The Bible refers to this expression in a number of different ways, in both the Old and New Testaments. The Day of the Lord is called *Great and Terrible* (Joel 2:31), the *Day of Vengeance* (Isaiah 61:2), the *Day of Visitation* (1 Peter 2:12), the *Day of Judgment* (1 John 4:17) and the *Great Day of God Almighty* (Revelation 16:14). Other passages simply refer to the Day of the Lord as simply *The Day*, *That Day*, or the *Day of God*.

The phrase The *Day of the Lord* is used often in the Old Testament (Isaiah 2:12, 13:6- 9; Ezekiel 13:5, 30:3; Joel 1:15, 2:1, 11, 31; 3:14; Amos 5:18,-20; Obadiah 15; Zephaniah 1:7,14; Zechariah 14:1; Malachi 4:5) and several times in the New Testament (Acts 2:20;   I Corinthians 5:5; II Corinthians 1:14; II Thessalonians 2:2; II Peter 3:10). Regardless of what it is called in scripture, when it is used in prophecy it is described as a day when God will bring his Wrath and righteous judgment against degenerate and unbelieving mankind. It will be a day when God will vanquish evil and purge the earth from all unbelievers. The phrase *Day of the Lord* refers to something that will take place at the end of the Church age…. more specifically, at the end of the *Great Tribulation*. Different prophecy teachers identify the Day of the Lord as a period of time…. Others as a single day. For example, in Chapter 1 a pre-wrath rapture was summarized that will take place between the 6th and 7th seal. The entire period of time which remains to the end of the Tribulation was called the *Day of the Lord* by Rosenthal and Van Kampen. Both had no choice but to also equate the Day of the Lord with the *Day of God's Wrath* because of Revelation 6:17 and the fact that they both assumed that the 7 Seals, the 7 Trumpets and the 7

Bowls occur in a serial sequence. We will show in Chapter 6 that this cannot be true. As discussed in Chapter 1, they also declared that the Rapture must occur between the 6th and 7th seal since they believed (correctly) that no Christian will ever experience the Wrath of God.

The key biblical verse which forms the foundation of a Pre-Wrath Rapture is Revelation 6:17, where John writes that: *the great **day** of his wrath is come; and who shall be able to stand?* We will now show that this **day** cannot be an extended period. It will become clear that the *Day of The Lord* is exactly what it says…. *a single day* on which the rapture will occur, but not between the 6th and 7th seal. It will also be proposed based upon scriptural evidence that there are *two* different end-time events which are both called the *Day of the Lord*, and they are separated by 1000 years (The Millennial Kingdom)

Perhaps the most graphic description of the *Day of the Lord* is found in the Old Testament in the Book of Zephaniah.

[14] *The great day of the LORD is near, it is near, and hastens greatly, even the voice of the* **Day of the Lord**: *the mighty man shall cry there bitterly.*
[**15**] *That day is* **a day of wrath, a day of trouble and distress, a day of wasteness and desolation, a day of darkness and gloominess, a day of clouds and thick darkness,**
[**16**] *A* **day of the trumpet** *and alarm against the fenced cities, and against the high towers.*
[**17**] *And I will bring distress upon men, that they shall walk like blind men, because they have sinned against the LORD: and their blood shall be poured out as dust, and their flesh as the dung.*
[**18**] *Neither their silver nor their gold shall be able to deliver them in the day of the LORD's wrath; but the* **whole land shall be devoured by the fire of his jealousy**: *for* **he shall make even a speedy riddance of all them that dwell in the land.**   Zephaniah 1: 14-18

Isaiah added some additional important information.

*And the destruction of the transgressors and of the sinners shall be together, and they that forsake the LORD **shall be consumed.** For the **Day of the LORD** of hosts shall be upon **every one that is proud and lofty**, and upon every one that is lifted up; and he shall be brought low* Isaiah 2:12

[4] *The noise of a multitude in the mountains, like as of a great people; a tumultuous noise of the kingdoms of **nations gathered together**: the* LORD of hosts musters the host of the battle.
[5] ***They come** from a far country, from the end of heaven, even the LORD, and the weapons of his indignation, **to destroy** the whole land.*
[6] *Howl ye; for the **Day of the Lord** is at hand; it shall come as a destruction from the Almighty.*
[7] *Therefore shall all hands be faint, and every man's heart shall melt:*
[8] *And they shall be afraid: pangs and sorrows shall take hold of them; they shall be in pain as a woman that travails: they shall be amazed one at another; **their faces shall be as flames**.*
[9] *Behold, the **Day of the LORD** cometh, cruel **both with wrath and fierce anger**, to lay the land desolate: and **He shall destroy the sinners thereof out of it.***
[10] *For the **stars of heaven** and the constellations thereof **shall not give their light**: the **sun shall be darkened** in his going forth, and the **moon shall not cause her light to shine**.*
[11] *And I will punish the world for their evil, and the wicked for their iniquity; and I will cause the arrogancy of the proud to cease, and will lay low the haughtiness of the terrible.*
[12] *I will make a man more precious than fine gold; even a man than the golden wedge of Ophir.*
[13] *Therefore **I will shake the heavens**, and **the earth shall remove out of her place**, in the wrath of the LORD of hosts, and in the Day of His Fierce Anger* Isaiah 13: 4-13

The last set of scriptures which we will examine are penned by the Prophet Joel

[12] *Let the heathen be wakened, and come up to the **Valley of Jehoshaphat**: for there will I sit to judge all the heathen round about.*
[13] ***Put ye in the sickle**, for the harvest is ripe: come, get you down; for the press is full, the fats overflow; for their wickedness is great.*
[14] *Multitudes, multitudes in the valley of decision: for the **Day of the LORD** is near in the valley of decision.*
[15] ***The sun and the moon shall be darkened**, and the **stars shall withdraw their shining**.*
[16] *The **LORD also shall roar out of Zion**, and utter his voice from Jerusalem; and the **heavens and the earth shall shake**: but the LORD will be the hope of his people, and the **strength of the children of Israel.***
[17] *So shall ye know that I am the LORD your God **dwelling in Zion**, my holy mountain: then shall Jerusalem be holy, and there shall no strangers pass through her any more*   Joel 3: 12-17

These Old Testament prophecies have several things in common.

(1)   The sun will be darkened, the moon will not reflect light and the stars will not shine
(2)   Sinners (not saints) will be destroyed
(3)   It will be a day of wrath, a day of trouble and distress, a day of waste and desolation
(4)   *Mountains and Islands* will all be moved/removed out of their place
(5)   This Day will be a conflict between the *Lord of Hosts* and all nations.

> ***Authors Comment**: The name Lord of Hosts occurs some 261 times in the Old Testament Scriptures. God is 1ˢᵗ called the Lord of Hosts (exactly) in I Samuel 1:3. The word hosts is a translation of the Hebrew word sabaoth, which means armies.*

(6)   The *Lord* will Roar out of Zion in the Day of the Lord

> ***Authors Comment**: Mt. Zion is a small hill about 50 Meters south west of the Temple Mount and Jerusalem. In Joel 3:16 Mount Zion is used*

metaphorically to refer to the heavenly Jerusalem, God's holy, eternal city. In Joel 3:16 the word *Lord* is used to reference Jesus Christ and not God the Father (Revelation 19).

There is enough evidence in all of these Old Testament scriptures to determine they are all referring to the *Battle of Armageddon*. The Battle of Armageddon will be on the last day of the current Church Age, and it will not take place until all of the 7 Bowl Judgments have been poured out upon all unbelievers. It is described by the apostle John in Revelation 19: 11-21.

[**10**] *And the fifth angel poured out his vial upon the seat of the beast; and his kingdom was full of* **darkness**
[**11**] *And blasphemed the God of heaven because of their pains and their sores, and repented not of their deeds.*
[**12**] *And the sixth angel poured out his vial upon the great river Euphrates; and the water thereof was dried up, that the way of the kings of the east might be prepared.*
[**13**] *And I saw three unclean spirits like frogs come out of the mouth of the dragon, and out of the mouth of the beast, and out of the mouth of the false prophet.*
[**14**] *For they are the spirits of devils, working miracles, which go forth unto the kings of the earth and of the whole world, to* **gather them to the battle of that great day of God Almighty**
 [**17**] *And the seventh angel poured out his vial into the air; and there came a great voice out of the temple of heaven, from the throne, saying:* **It is done**.
[**18**] *And there were voices, and* **thunders, and lightnings***; and* **there was a great earthquake***, such as was not since men were upon the earth, so mighty an earthquake, and so great*   Revelation 16: 10, 17-18

Authors Comment: Compare Revelation 16:18 to Revelation 6:12

The **Day of the Lord** in the Old Testament can be compared to what Jesus Christ revealed to His apostles concerning His 2^{cd} Advent (return to earth) in Matthew 24 (The Olivet Discourse).

[**29**] *Immediately **after** the tribulation of those days shall the **sun be darkened**, and the **moon shall not give her light**, and **the stars shall fall from heaven**, and the powers of the heavens shall be shaken*
[**30**] *And **then shall appear the sign of the Son of man in heaven**: and then shall all the tribes of the earth mourn, and **they shall see the Son of man coming in the clouds of heaven with power and great glory.***
[**31**] *And he shall send his angels with a great sound of **a trumpet**, and **they shall gather together his elect** from the four winds, from one end of heaven to the other.*   Matthew 24: 29-31

[**14**] *And this **gospel of the kingdom shall be preached in all the world** for a witness unto all nations; and **then shall the end come*** (see Rev 14:6)
[**15**] *When ye therefore shall see the abomination of desolation, spoken of by Daniel the prophet, stand in the holy place, (whoso readeth, let him understand:)*
[**16**] *Then let them which be in Judaea flee into the mountains*
Revelation 14: 14-16   (See Revelation 12: 6, 13)

    Authors Comment: There will be two unmistakable and significant signs that the *Great Tribulation is about to begin*. The Great Tribulation will *begin* when Satan is cast out of heaven by Michael and his holy angels (Revelation 12: 3-4). When this happens, a remnant of the Jews will flee to the mountains…. probably in Petra (Revelation 12: 6, 14, 17. The city of Petra is not mentioned in the Bible except by its Hebrew name, *Sela* (Isaiah 16:1 and 2 Kings 14:7) which means *rock* (See Psalms 18:2). Satan will be furious and he will pursue the fleeing remnant to destroy them all (Revelation 12: 14-15). As Satan is about to destroy them, God intervenes and saves His people (Revelation 12:16). Satan will then turn back and attack

Jerusalem. He will conquer parts of the city and assume control of the newly built temple. He will sit in the Holy place and rule (II Thessalonians 2: 3-4). Anyone who does not bow down to him and worship him will be killed (Revelation 13: 14-15). This desecration of the Holy temple is called *the abomination that causes desolation* (Matthew 24:14-15, Daniel 12:11). Note that this cannot occur unless the Temple is rebuilt (compare to Revelation 11: 1-2). When this takes place, the 7 Trumpet Judgments will begin. The *7 Trumpet Judgments* are the *Wrath of Satan* (Revelation 12:12)

[21] *For **then shall be great tribulation**, such as was not since the beginning of the world to this time, no, nor ever shall be.*
[22] *And **except those days should be shortened**, there should no flesh be saved: but for the elect's sake those days shall be shortened.*
Matthew 24: 21-22

> **Authors Comment**: Once the *Tribulation* has begun it will last until Satan is defeated at the Battle of Armageddon. It should be noted here that this is *proof* that the period of *great persecution* by Satan, the Antichrist and the False Prophet *cannot* last more than 1260 days (Revelation 12:6) or about 3.5 years (See Phillips: *The Daniel 70 Week Prophecy* for complete proof of this statement). This does not preclude the Tribulation lasting a total of 7 years as all Pre-tribulation teachers claim. In this case, the 1st 3.5 years are generally considered to be a period of time over which the Seals 1-3 are removed and no Wrath is brought out of heaven

Jesus Christ spoke the following prophecies to his 12 disciples just before He was arrested on the Mount of Olives.

[29] *Immediately **after the tribulation of those days** shall the sun be darkened, and the moon shall not give her light, and the stars shall fall from heaven, and the powers of the heavens shall be shaken:*
[30] *And **then** shall appear the sign of the Son of man in heaven: and*

then shall all the tribes of the earth mourn, and they shall see the Son of man coming in the clouds of heaven with power and great glory.
[31] ***And he shall send his angels with a great sound of a trumpet, and they shall gather together his elect from the four winds, from one end of heaven to the other.*** Matthew 24: 29-31

This is a clear and unambiguous statement by Jesus Christ in Matthew 24 that the Rapture will not occur until *after* Great Tribulation (Matthew 24:29). We will show beyond any reasonable doubt in Chapter 4 that Christ in His mercy has not destined the Church to go through all of the Great Tribulation, but the Rapture of all living believers will take place 10 days before the Church age ends and will immediately precede the 7 Bowl Judgments of *God's Wrath*. It is proposed that the *Rapture* will take place on the *Feast of Trumpets,* Tishri 1. This is the *shortening of time* referred to by Christ in Matthew 24:22. The *Battle of Armageddon* will take place 10 days later on Nisan 15 on the Feast of *Yom Kippur*.

> ***Authors Comment***: In His great Olivet Discourse when Christ revealed to His 12 disciples the ultimate destiny of the Jews, He was referring to all Jews and Gentiles who had accepted Him as their Lord and savior and were still alive when the Great Tribulation begins. He ***did not*** promise that those believers would escape *all* of the tribulation and wrath of the great tribulation, but He did promise all believers that:

[21] *For **then** shall be great tribulation, such as was not since the beginning of the world to this time, no, nor ever shall be.*
[22] *And **except those days should be shortened**, there should no flesh be saved: but for the elect's sake those days shall be shortened*
Matthew 24: 21-22

> ***Authors Comment***: Why would Jesus Christ tell His disciples that Tribulation was coming upon the entire world if no believer would ever have to experience tribulation? (Pre-Tribulation Rapture). To the contrary, He wanted all of His believers to be prepared. However, in His mercy he would

shorten those days for His *elect*. What God did promise by the Apostle Paul that no Christian would ever experience the *Wrath of God*, which are the 7 Bowl Judgments (Revelation 15:1, Revelation 16:1). We will show later that the 7 Bowls will be poured out over a period of 10 days between the Jewish *Feast of Trumpets* on Tishri 1 and the Jewish *Feast of Yom Kippur* on Tishri 10. The *Rapture* will occur on the Feast of Trumpets to remove all of God's elect (Jews and Gentiles) from His Wrath. This gathering together of His elect is what we call the *Rapture.* Note according to Christ' own words this is *after* the tribulation (Matthew 24: 29-31). We will discuss this in Chapter 3. Note that according to His own words this is not a Post-Tribulation rapture because Christ also revealed that: except those days should be *shortened,* there should no flesh be saved: but for the elect's sake those days shall be shortened (Matthew 22:24). The total length of the Great Tribulation would not be shortened, only the length of time that the elect would have to spend in the tribulation period (3.5 years-10 days).

It is with a great deal of certainty that we equate the *Day of the Lord* with the *Battle of Armageddon*

> **Isaiah 24:21-22**
>
> So it will happen in that day,
> That the LORD will punish the host of heaven on high,
> And the kings of the earth on earth.
> They will be gathered together
> Like prisoners in the dungeon,
> And will be confined in prison;
> And after many days they will be punished.

and that both the day of the Lord and the Battle of Armageddon occur immediately following the 7 Bowl Judgments of God's Wrath.

Chapter 3

The Day of Jesus Christ

In Chapter 2 it was shown that the Day of the Lord is the *Battle of Armageddon.* This battle is described in Revelation 19: 11-21. It is well known that the Battle of Armageddon will be fought by Jesus Christ. This marks His 2nd advent and it appears that He will be accompanied by His angels and the resurrected/raptured saints (Daniel 12:10, Rev 3:18).

[**13**] *And he was clothed with a vesture dipped in blood: and his name is called The Word of God.*
[**14**] *And the armies which were in heaven **followed him upon white horses, clothed in fine linen, white and clean***   Revelation 19: 13-14

So, why is this called the Day of the Lord? In the Old Testament, Jesus Christ is not identified as the Conquering King because His name never appeared in the Old Testament. However, New Testament saints know that the Battle of Armageddon is to be fought by our Lord Jesus Christ (Revelation 19). Jesus Christ is our Lord and Savior (Revelation 17:14).

The *Day of the Lord* is very different from the *Day of Jesus Christ.* The day of Jesus Christ was revealed to both Jews and Gentiles by the Apostle Paul in his letter to the Church at Corinth.

[**4**] *I thank my God always on your behalf, for the grace of God which is given you by Jesus Christ;*
[**5**] *That in everything ye are enriched by him, in all utterance, and in all knowledge;*
[**6**] *Even as the testimony of Christ was confirmed in you:*
[**7**] *So that ye come behind in no gift; waiting for the **coming of our***

Lord *Jesus Christ:*

[8] *Who shall also confirm you unto the end, that ye may be blameless in the **Day of our Lord Jesus Christ**.*   I Corinthians 1: 4-8

The Apostle Paul is not referring of the Battle of Armageddon but to the Rapture of the saints. We know this for certain, since he states that this day is for those who wait for our Lord Jesus Christ (I Corinthians 1:7). Those who will Christ engage at the Battle of Armageddon are all unbelievers.

The Rapture will occur before the great Battle of Armageddon, at the last trump. The apostle Paul revealed much of what we know about the Rapture in his epistles.

[15] *For this we say unto you by the word of the Lord, that we which are alive and remain unto the coming of the Lord shall not prevent them which are asleep.*

[16] *For the Lord himself shall descend from heaven with a shout, with the voice of the archangel, and **with the trump of God**: and the dead in Christ shall rise first:*

[17] ***Then we which are alive and remain shall be caught up together with them in the clouds**, to meet the Lord in the air: and so shall we ever be with the Lord.*

[18] *Wherefore comfort one another with these words.*
I Thessalonians 4: 14-18

[51] *Behold, I shew you a **mystery**; We shall not all sleep, but we shall all be changed,*

[52] *In a moment, in the twinkling of an eye, **at the last trump**: for the trumpet shall sound, and the dead shall be raised incorruptible, and we shall be changed.*

[53] ***For this corruptible must put on incorruption**, and this mortal must put on immortality.*

[54] *So when this corruptible shall have put on incorruption, and this mortal shall have put on immortality, then shall be brought to pass the*

saying that is written, Death is swallowed up in victory.
[55] O death, where is thy sting? O grave, where is thy victory?
[56] The sting of death is sin; and the strength of sin is the law.
[57] But thanks be to God, which giveth us the victory through our Lord Jesus Christ.
[58] Therefore, my beloved brethren, be ye steadfast, unmovable, always abounding in the work of the Lord, forasmuch as ye know that your labor is not in vain in the Lord.   I Corinthians 15: 51-58

The issue of the Rapture is not that it **will** take place, but **when** will it take place. Christ told His disciples:

*[29] Immediately **after the tribulation** of those days shall the **sun be darkened, and the moon shall not give her light, and the stars shall fall from heaven, and the powers of the heavens shall be shaken:***
*[30] And **then** shall appear the sign of the Son of man in heaven: and then shall all the tribes of the earth mourn, and they shall see the Son of man coming in the clouds of heaven with power and great glory.*
*[31] And **He shall send his angels with a great sound of a trumpet**, and **they shall gather together his elect** from the four winds, from one end of heaven to the other*   Matthew 24: 29-31

It was always a mystery to me personally that the issue of when the Rapture would take place was such a hotly debated issue. Jesus Christ stated without any ambiguity that the Rapture would not take place until *after the tribulation* and *multiple celestial signs* take place.

This does not mean that it might be the last event of the tribulation, but that it would be very near the end. In Chapter 3 we will show beyond reasonable doubt that the *Rapture* will occur on the Feast of Trumpets, Tishri 1, after the 7th Trumpet has been sounded, and that the *Battle of Armageddon* will be fought ten days later on the Jewish Feast of Yom Kippur, Tishri 10. How can we be sure that the Rapture will take place on the Feast of Trumpets and the Battle of Armageddon on the Feast of

Yom Kippur? In Chapter 4 we will summarize the 7 Feasts of Israel and show that this is highly likely.

The Day of the Lord: *Revisited*

The 12 disciples were told by Jesus Christ to preach the Gospel and spread the New Covenant (salvation by faith and grace) to the Jews (Matthew 10:5). They were all anointed by Christ and each was given power by the Holy Ghost to preach, teach and heal all over the known world. The New Covenant which was ratified by Christ on the Cross of Calvary was offered first to the Jews. On the Day of Pentecost, 50 days after Christ was Resurrected, The Holy Spirit fell upon the Jews who had come from all over the world to observe Pentecost (Acts 2: 1-5). The Holy Ghost fell upon all who would turn to Jesus Christ as their long-awaited Messiah. On that day, there were 3000 Jews that accepted Christ and were saved. These converts would join the existing 120 Jews who had already accepted Christ as Lord and Savior (Acts 1: 15-16) and the 12 disciples who were called the *little flock* of Jesus Christ (Luke 12:32).

Although 3000 Jews accepted Christ on the Feast of Pentecost, the Jewish spiritual leaders and the majority of Jews would not accept the free gift of eternal life. Unbelief and hatred finally came to a head a short time later. Steven delivered his great sermon to the Jews trying to save their souls, but when he had finished, he was stoned to death in Jerusalem (Acts 7-8). God had finally had enough, and from that point on He turned to the Gentiles to spread the Gospel to Jews and Gentiles alike. Saul of Tarsus (Paul) was chosen by God to evangelize the Gentiles 1st and then the Jews (Ephesians 3:8). The other 12 disciples were chosen to go to the Jews (Galatians 2: 7-8).

There are 27 books in the New Testament, and Paul wrote at least 13. Paul wrote letters to the Gentile churches which he founded in Asia (Asia Minor) which formed 13 Chapters of the New Testament. The

Apostles or other anointed believers wrote the other 14 or 13 books in the New Testament.

Another Day of the Lord?

The Book of II Peter was written by the apostle Peter who was the chief apostle sent by Jesus Christ to the Jews (Galatians 2:8). The authorship of II Peter has been questioned, although since it was adopted as scriptural cannon, we should accept the author as Peter. In II Peter, the author devotes a portion of scripture to the fate of the Jews and the earth in general.

[4] *...where is the promise of his coming? for since the fathers fell asleep, all things continue as they were from the beginning of the creation.*
[5] *For this they willingly are ignorant of, that by the word of God the heavens were of old, and the earth standing out of the water and in the water:*
[6] *Whereby **the world that then was**, being overflowed with water, **perished**:*
[7] *But **the heavens and the earth**, which are now, by the same word are kept in store, **reserved unto fire** against the day of judgment and perdition of ungodly men.*
[8] *But, beloved, be not ignorant of this one thing, that **one day is with the Lord as a thousand years**, and a thousand years as one day.*
[9] *The Lord is not slack concerning his promise, as some men count slackness; but is longsuffering to us-ward, not willing that any should perish, but that all should come to repentance.*
[10] *But the **Day of the Lord** will come as a thief in the night; in **the which the heavens shall pass away** with a great noise, and the **elements shall melt with fervent heat**, the **earth** also and the works that are therein **shall be burned up**.*
[11] *Seeing then that all these things shall be dissolved, what manner of persons ought ye to be in all holy conversation and godliness,*

[**12**] *Looking for and hasting unto the coming of the day of God, wherein* ***the heavens being on fire shall be dissolved,*** *and the* ***elements shall melt with fervent heat****?*   II Peter 3: 4-12

Peter wrote both I Peter and II Peter while in Rome just before he was martyred. Some say that another person actually wrote II Peter for Peter while he was in prison. Regardless of where the actual written text came from, the authenticity of II Peter by the apostle was never questioned by the church fathers and it was accepted as canon. Chapter 3 of II Peter deals largely with what Peter calls the *Day of the Lord*. We have identified the *Day of the Lord* in other Old and New Testament sources as referring to the *Battle of Armageddon*. In doing so, the Holy Scriptures were allowed to simply speak for themselves. In II Peter 3: 4-12, we find some things which do not quite agree with previous references to the Day of the Lord.

Peter opens with a short discourse on how unbelievers simply ignore the words of Christ and His apostles that a day of reckoning is coming in which all unbelievers will be destroyed just as at Sodom and Gomorrha. Unbelievers say: "all things are just as they always were; Where is the promise of His coming?" (II Peter 2:6, II Peter 3:5). Peter then wrote that the earth would once again, one day, be purged of all sin and sinners by fire (II Peter 3:7). He then made reference to a thousand years being as a single day to God (II Peter 3:9). This is a secondary reference that is generally believed to mean that this earth will last 7000 years (7 days of 1000 years/day) until it is renovated and purged of all sin. The 7th and last 1000-year period of time is the 1000-year *Millennial Kingdom* during which Christ will reign and the Jews will inherit and live in the Promised Land. These 1000 years will start *after* the *Battle of Armageddon.* Paul then identifies a *Day of the Lord* in which the earth will be completely destroyed by fire, the heavens will pass away and the elements will melt in great heat. These things which will happen are quite different from what will take place at the Battle of Armageddon.

When Christ returns to fight the Battle of Armageddon, there will be some geographical changes; but nothing of this magnitude. When Christ returns in His 2nd advent, He will descend to the Mt. of Olives and His feet will split the Mount. Following the Battle of Armageddon, the Land of Israel will be leveled into a great plane, and Jerusalem will be lifted up to form a high plateau where Christ will rule and reign for 1000 years (Phillips, The Millennial Kingdom: *Life After the Great Tribulation*). All of these changes will be geographical and none will be worldwide. The events surrounding II Peter 3: 4-12 will be worldwide and even celestial. Is there any event which could qualify as this *Day of the Lord*? *Yes*, there is!

After the Battle of Armageddon takes place and the Feast of Tabernacles is held in Jerusalem, the 1000-year Millennial Kingdom will begin. After the Battle, Satan will be bound in chains and cast into the *bottomless pit* (Revelation 20: 1-3). After the 1000 years have passed, Satan will be released from his subterranean dungeon and he will once again assemble all unbelievers to attack Jerusalem for the 3rd time (Revelation 20: 7-9). We will call this *Satans Last Stand*. Satan will assemble his followers once again just north of Jerusalem, but the assault on Jerusalem will never begin. It is not commonly recognized by most Christians, but **God** Himself will quickly destroy Satan and his evil forces with *fire* from heaven (Revelation 20:9). Satan will be cast into the *Lake of Burning Fire* (Revelation 20:10), and those who followed him …. whose names are not written in the *Book of Life*…. will be Judged at the *Great White Throne Judgment*. They will be condemned to everlasting punishment in the Lake of Burning Fire (Revelation 20: 11-15). After these things, John sees a New Heaven and a New Earth (Revelation 21:1). The present heavens and earth will be purified and cleansed by fire; just as Pete predicted (II Peter 3:10). This sequence of events perfectly fit the prophecies in II Peter 3: 4-12. It can be proposed with conviction that this is the **Day of the Lord** spoken of by Peter in II Peter 3:10. This is most appropriate: After all, it was by the power of God that the heavens and earth were created, and it should be God who creates a new heaven and a new earth. *The Kingdom of God* had now come. So, what is this Day of the Lord that the Apostle Peter is referring to?

The conclusion is that Paul is not describing the Battle of Armageddon, but a Day after the 1000-year Millennial Kingdom when Satan and all sin will be removed from this earth. The earth will be renovated by fire and the heavens reformed (Revelation 21: 1-7).

This conclusion firmly supports that there are two that are consistently identified as the Lord, and that there are two separated Days of the Lord described in the New Testament. One will be at the Battle of Armageddon (The 2nd advent of Jesus Christ) and the other at the end of the 1000-year Millennial Kingdom (God the Father).

Chapter 4 will now show the most likely scenario for *when* the Battle of Armageddon and the Rapture will take place.

Chapter 4

The Seven Seals

An overwhelming majority of biblical scholars teach that the 7 Seals, the 7 Trumpets and the 7 Bowls are executed *sequentially* over a 7-year

Figure 1

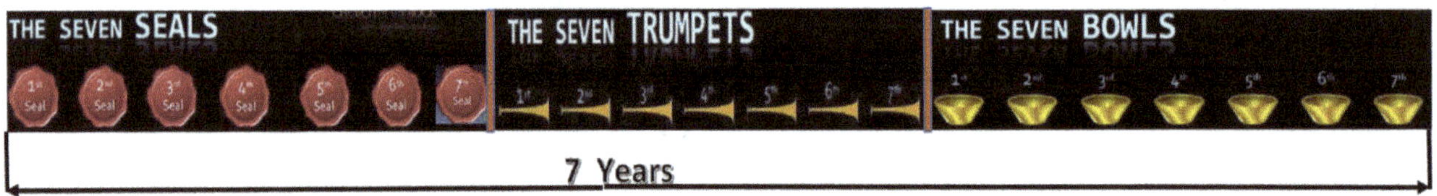

period of time. The duration of each set will depend upon which article or book one reads and who is the author(s). The following two scenarios are typical and illustrative.

Figure 2

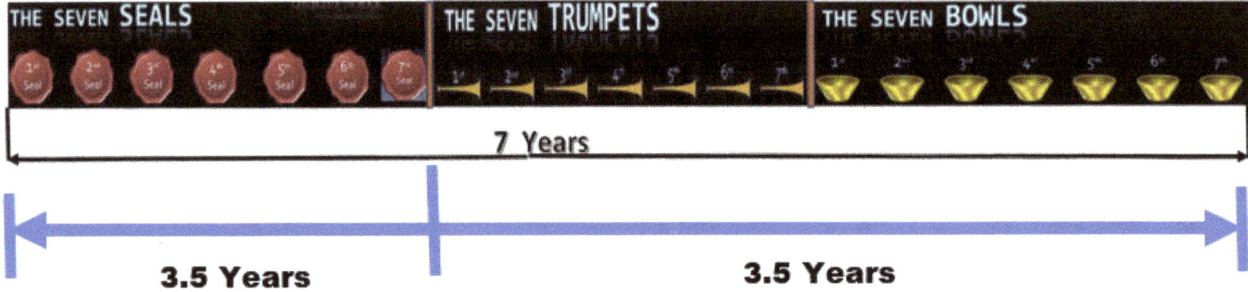

Figure 3

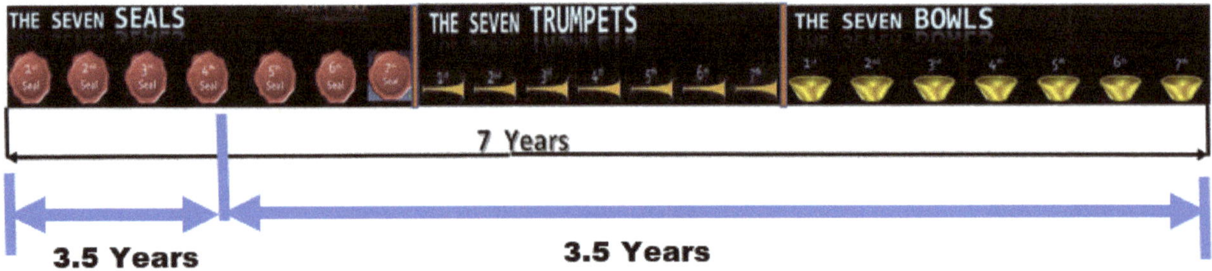

The 1st four seals are almost always placed during the first 3.5 years of the Tribulation period. The 1st three seals represent conditions that one might expect when war and conflict break out. The 4th seal is more specific. Death rides a pale horse followed

by Hades. The 4th Seal predicts that ¼ of all people upon the earth will

perish. It is not clear if this will take place only in the days after the 4th seal is removed, or as a consequence of the accumulated impact of Seals 1-4. It is likely the former.

Seal 5 is a scene of those who have been martyred for Christ. They are seen beneath the throne of God (Revelation 6: 9-10), and they cry out for vengeance. God gives each one a white robe and tells them to wait awhile… until more of their brothers must be killed.

Seal 6 will prove to be extremely important.

[12] *And I beheld when he had opened the sixth seal, and, lo, there was a great earthquake; and the sun became black as sackcloth of hair, and the moon became as blood;*

[13] *And the stars of heaven fell unto the earth, even as a fig tree casts her untimely figs, when she is shaken of a mighty wind.*

[14] *And the heaven departed as a scroll when it is rolled together; and every mountain and island were moved out of their places.*

[**15**] *And the kings of the earth, and the great men, and the rich men, and the chief captains, and the mighty men, and every bondman, and every free man, hid themselves in the dens and in the rocks of the mountains;*
[**16**] *And said to the mountains and rock: Fall on us, and hide us from the face of him that sits on the throne, and from the wrath of the Lamb:*
[**17**] *For the great day of his wrath is come; and who shall be able to stand?*   Revelation 6: 12-17

When the 6th Seal is removed: (1) There is a great earthquake (2) The sun turns black and the moon turns red (3) The heavens depart as a scroll is rolled up (4) Every mountain and every island are moved out of their place (5) The Kings of the earth hide in rocks and caves because (6) The Wrath of God has come.

When the 7th seal is removed, there is complete silence in heaven for about half an hour. Clearly, something is about to happen that stuns all of the creatures and angels which surround the Throne of God. They all fall silent because the scroll can now be unrolled and the 7 trumpets and 7 Bowls can now be described.

Notice that when the 6th Seal is removed John, records that ***The Wrath of God*** has come. Read these verses (Revelation 6: 1-17) very carefully…. Study them and memorize what will happen as each of the 7 seals are removed. The following analysis will challenge all you may have been told about the sequential nature of the 7 Seals, the 7 Trumpets and the 7 Bowls.

The vast majority of all prophecy teachers, pastors and scholars will resolutely declare that: (1) The 7 Seals, 7 Trumpets and 7 Bowl Judgments are serial in nature, and once the 1st Seal is removed, all 21 events will occur in sequence (2) The Rapture of all saints (dead or alive) is assumed by most to be a *Pre-tribulation Rapture*. What does this mean? It means that the Rapture will take place before any of the 7 seals will be removed by Christ, and that all 21 events occur in a serial sequence. We will now prove that this is incorrect and untenable theology.

The 7 Seals: *Correct Chronology*

The 7 Seals are broken to gain access to the contents of a large scroll which belong to God. It contains a description of what will occur as the Church Age draws to a close, and what will happen both during and after the 1000-year Millennial Kingdom. It will be shown that as each of the 6 seals are removed, John saw visions of the future which would later be fulfilled. Seals 1-4 only predict *conditions;* Seal 5 reveals that martyrs are beneath the Throne of God crying for vengeance and Seal 6 predicts a series of *specific* events which will later take place in the latter days of the Great Tribulation. Seal 7 is a 30-minute period of heavenly silence.

Note that the 7 trumpets and the 7 Bowls are each delivered to the earth from heaven by mighty angels at the command of God (Revelation 8:2, Revelation 15:1). The 7 seals are broken and removed by Jesus Christ (Revelation 5:5). Even though there is a direct relationship between the seals, bowls and trumpets…there is a distinct difference between the Seals, Trumpets and Bowls. The 7 seals only *reveal* things to come: The 7 Trumpets and the 7 Bowls actually *cause* things to happen. The seals are 7 in number and they have been placed upon a royal document called a *scroll*. The scroll was being kept by God, and when it came time to reveal its contents only Christ was worthy to reveal its mysteries

(Revelation 5: 1-8). John was actually to *see* visions of its contents as it is unrolled. This scroll contains the eternal plan of God to: (1) Complete the full Body of all true believers who have accepted Christ as their Lord and savior during the Church Age and (2) Fulfill all of His covenant promises to the nation of Israel. He had promised His beloved nation of Israel that one day He would place them in the land of promise and that they would dwell there. This *unconditional* covenant promise of God will be fulfilled in the 1000-year Millennial Kingdom. The purpose of the Great

Tribulation is to fully restore the Jews into an intimate and personal relationship with God as He intended all along. Only God can do this, and He will do it to exalt and honor His Son Jesus Christ.

[18] *But those things, which God before had showed by the mouth of all his prophets, that Christ should suffer, he hath so fulfilled.*
[19] *Repent ye therefore, and be converted, that your sins may be blotted out, when the times of refreshing shall come from the presence of the Lord;*
[20] *And he shall send Jesus Christ, which before was preached unto you:*

[21] Whom *the heaven must receive until the times of restitution of all things, which God hath spoken by the mouth of all his holy prophets since the world began* Acts 3: 18-21

As Christ begins to remove the 7 seals, John is shown what will take place as this *Church Age* comes to an end. The first vision comes as the 1st seal is removed.

[1] *And I saw when the Lamb opened one of the seals, and I heard, as it were the noise of thunder, one of the four beasts saying, Come and see.*
[2] *And I saw, and behold a white horse: and he that sat on him had a bow; and a crown was given unto him: and he went forth conquering, and to conquer* Revelation 6: 1-2

As Christ breaks the 1st seal, one of the 4 beasts that stand before the throne of God tells John: *Come and see* (Revelation 6:1). As John obeys, he sees a white horse and a rider which has a bow but no arrows. The rider comes forth to conquer (Revelation 6:2). This rider has long been debated. Many have identified the rider of this horse as Jesus Christ, but this is entirely out of context with the horses that will appear as Seals 2-4 are broken. This rider has a bow but no arrows: He will conquer with military power as well as political cunning. It is not Jesus Christ who rides forth on a white horse. It is not exclusively Satan, and in context with the other three riders it cannot be only the Antichrist. All 4 horses and riders personify and represent both supernatural and devastating forces that will be at work during the Great Tribulation. After careful consideration, it is suggested and concluded that this rider represents political and military power of Satan during the Great Tribulation. Satan will conquer by using the military power of the final 10-nation confederacy (Daniel 7, Revelation 13). His instruments of power and destruction will be the Antichrist and the False prophet (Revelation 13: 1-18).

For there shall arise false Christs, and false prophets, and shall shew great signs and wonders; insomuch that, if it were possible, they shall deceive the very elect.   Matthew 24:24

The Antichrist, False Prophet and Satan will fulfil these words of Christ. They will deceive many, and condemn those who reject Christ as their Lord and Savior to everlasting judgment in the Lake of Fire. This will be manifested throughout the duration of the Great Tribulation accompanied by what each of the first 4 seals predict: *Destruction, Wars, Famine*, and *Death*.

 As the second seal is broken/removed, John is again commanded to *come and see,* and he sees a rider on a Red Horse.

Second Seal
Rider on Red Horse

Rider has a Great Sword
Rider has power to take Peace from World

Revelatiion 6: 3-4

[3] *And when he had opened the second seal, I heard the second beast say, Come and see.*
[4] *And there went out another horse that was red: and power was given to him that sat thereon to take peace from the earth, and that they should kill one another: and there was given unto him a great sword*

Revelation 6: 3-4

This rider is given a *great sword*. This sword represents the instrument by which peace will be removed from all of the earth. Men will war against one another and kill one another. *Is this horse and great sword the only instrument of war*? Likely not. In the 1st century there were no helicopters, tanks or airplanes and John is conveying the instruments of war which will be used over 2000 years later as best he can. It is better to interpret the sword which takes peace from the world as a symbol of destruction and death over an extended period of time…. characterized by conflict, terror and bloodshed. The fact that there have been wars and rumers of wars throughout recorded history cannot be challenged. However, the prophetic nature of the scroll demands that this imagery applies to a future period of death and destruction that will surpass anything yet recorded in history. In fact, everything in the Book of Revelation from Chapter 4 -Chapter 22 is yet future. The 3rd seal is now removed

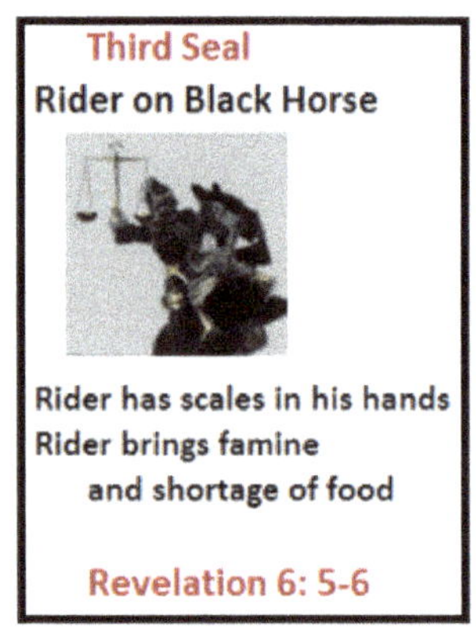

[5] *And when he had opened the third seal, I heard the third beast say, Come and see. And I beheld, and lo a black horse; and he that sat on him had a pair of balances in his hand.*
[6] *And I heard a voice in the midst of the four beasts say, A measure of wheat for a penny, and three measures of barley for a penny; and see thou hurt not the oil and the wine*   Revelation 6: 5-6

When Jesus Christ opens the 3rd seal. John is told to *come and see* A black horse appears with a rider which has a scale in his right hand. This scale is one which was commonly used to weigh grain. A counterweight was used to determine the purchase price. The rider clothed in black and the scales indicate that a time is coming of sorrow and suffering due to a shortage and scarcity of food. *What could cause such a worldwide lack of food?*

This is a prediction of what will start when Trump 1 and 2 sounds, and will be completed when the 7 Bowl Judgments are unleashed upon the earth. When Trump 1 sounds *all* green grass is burned up along with 1/3 of all the trees (Revelation 8:7). If something burns up *all* the green grass, crops and trees will largely be burned up also. There will not only be devastating fires, but when the 3rd trumpet sounds, 1/3 of all the fresh water will be polluted in some way (Revelation 8:10). The devastation of crops and food when Trump 1 and Trump 2 are blown is bad enough, but later when the 3rd Bowl is poured out, *all* fresh water (rivers, streams and water wells) turn to blood. The 3rd Bowl in a sequence of seven will obviously be poured out upon all the earth very near the end of the Tribulation period. Man can be denied food for an extended period of time, but water is necessary to sustain life. Medical research has determined that the average person can live only 3-4 days without water. With access to only bottled water, mankind would only survive days. The 4th seal is now removed.

[7] *And when he had opened the fourth seal, I heard the voice of the fourth beast say, Come and see.*
[8] *And I looked, and behold a pale horse: and his name that sat on him was Death, and Hell followed with him. And power was given unto them over the fourth part of the earth, to kill with sword, and with hunger, and with death, and with the beasts of the earth* Revelation 6: 7-8

As the 4th seal is broken, John turns to see a pale horse. In Greek, the phrase translated as pale horse (KJV) means a sickly, yellowish-green color. The rider of this horse is *death*. The 1st seal has brought deception by force or cunning. The 2nd Seal brings war....and war always brings famine and devastation. The 3rd Seal predicts severe *worldwide* poverty and famine. The 4th scal reveals a pale horse, and it its rider is *death*. ¼ of all the world's population will die. War and famine always result in death. This is a serious revelation of what is about to take place as the Great Tribulation is about to begin. The 5th Seal is now removed.

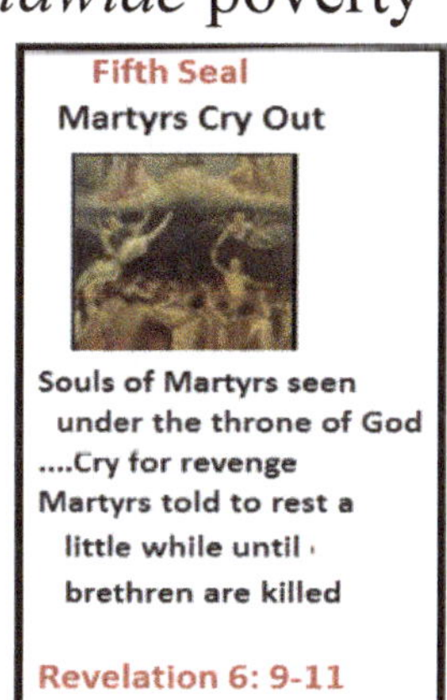

[9] *And when he had opened the fifth seal, I saw under the altar the souls of them that were slain for the word of God, and for the testimony which they held:*

*[10] And they cried with a loud voice, saying, How long, O Lord, holy
and true, dost thou not judge and avenge our blood on them that dwell
on the earth?*
*[11] And white robes were given unto every one of them; and it was said
unto them, that they should rest yet for a little season, until their fellow-
servants also and their brethren, that should be killed as they were,
should be fulfilled*   Revelation 6: 9-11

Be sure about it......the 4th seal did not cause these things to happen
......they will take place as the 7 Trumpets and the 7 Bowls take place
over the last 3.5 years of the Church Age.

As the 5th seal is broken, John is shown a remarkable vision concerning
the Christians who have been martryed rather than deny Jesus Christ.
The death and destruction predicted as the first four seals are broken will
prove to be the ultimate test of faith to many Christians who will not
bow down to the Antichrist. Many will not publicly deny their faith in
Christ and be put to death (Revelation 13: 14-15). Once again, it should
be clear that the opening of the 5th seal is not an *event* that will happen
all at once, but something that will happen *throughout the duration* of
the last 3.5 years of this age. This is a remarkable prophecy.... the souls
of all faithful martyrs are seen *beneath the throne of God* (Revelation 6:
9-11). Their suffering and faith to the death is evidently so great that
when they are martyred for Christ they are immediately taken to a place
beneath the heavenly throne of God. They cry out for vengeance:

*And they cried with a loud voice, saying, how long, O Lord, holy and
true, dost thou not judge and avenge our blood on them that dwell on the
earth?*   Revelation 6:10

The response to this plea is both revealing and immediate.

*And white robes were given unto every one of them; and it was said unto
them, that they should rest yet for a little season, until their fellow*

servants also and their brethren, that should be killed as they were, should be fulfilled   Revelation 6:11

This scene is captured completely by the words of Robert L. Thomas.

> These words were spoken by Jesus Christ to the souls under God's throne. These words give them complete assurance that He will avenge their blood, but the time has not yet arrived for the culmination of that vengeance. There must still be others who will be tested, tried and martyred for Christ. Death will take an even greater toll on those on the earth before Christ returns. Until then, those who have already been martyred can rest in the assurance that they will be avenged and attain eternal life.

A question which must be asked is: *From what dispensation of time did these martyrs come from?* Revelation 6:9 tells us that: *I saw under the altar the souls of them that were slain for the word of God, and for the testimony which they held.* This seems to indicate that these martyrs come from when Adam fell to the 2nd advent of Christ. Men of God, prophets in the Old Testament, and New Testament witnesses for Jesus Christ have been slain through recorded time. This holy and blameless group of martyrs will not be complete until the 3.5 years of Satans reign of terror have come to an end. It appears that they will be raised in a special resurrection just before the 1000 Millennial kingdom begins.

...and I saw the souls of them that were beheaded for the witness of Jesus, and for the word of God, and which had not worshipped the beast, neither his image, neither had received his mark upon their foreheads, or in their hands; and they lived and reigned with Christ a thousand years.   Revelation 20: 4b

We have shown mounting evidence that the 7 seals are not in lock-step with the 7 Trumpets and 7 Bowls, but they only prophecy and overview things which will take place during the last 3.5 years of the Church Age. The seals consume no time and do not precede the Trumpet or Bowl

Judgments in lock-step time delays as is commonly taught. When the 6th seal is broken *possibility* becomes *certainty*.

[**12**] *And I beheld when he had opened the sixth seal, and, lo, there was a great earthquake; and the sun became black as sackcloth of hair, and the moon became as blood;*
[**13**] *And the stars of heaven fell unto the earth, even as a fig tree casts her untimely figs, when she is shaken of a mighty wind.*
[**14**] *And the **heaven departed as a scroll when it is rolled together; and every mountain and island were moved out of their places***
Revelation 6: 12-14

When the 6th seal is broken unprecedented heaven and earthly disturbances are prophesied. (1) The sun becomes black (2) The moon turns blood red (3) Stars fall from the sky (4) Heaven rolls up like a scroll. *When do these things occur in the Period of Great Tribulation?*

This question was answered by the prophet Joel.

[**1**] *Blow ye the trumpet in Zion, and sound an alarm in my holy mountain: let all the inhabitants of the land tremble: for the **Day of the LORD** cometh, for it is nigh at hand;*
[**2**] ***A Day** of **darkness and of gloominess**, **a day** of clouds and of thick darkness, as the morning spread upon the mountains: a great people and a strong; there hath not been ever the like, neither shall be any more after it, even to the years of many generations*   Joel 2: 1-2

[**2**] *I will also gather all nations, and will bring them down into the **Valley of Jehoshaphat**, and will plead with them there for my people*

and for my heritage Israel, whom they have scattered among the nations, and parted my land. Joel 3:2

[14] *Multitudes, multitudes in the **valley of decision**: for the **Day of the LORD** is near in the valley of decision.*
[15] The sun and the moon shall be darkened, and the stars shall withdraw their shining.
[16] *The LORD also shall roar out of Zion, and utter his voice from Jerusalem; **and the heavens and the earth shall shake**: but the LORD will be the hope of his people, and the strength of the children of Israel.* Joel 3: 14-16

Joel clearly says that a ***Day of the Lord*** is coming and that it will be a day of darkness and gloom. A day of earthquakes, and a day in which the sun will be darkened and the stars cease to shine. There can be no doubt that this Day of the Lord is the ***Battle of Armageddon*** (Compare Joel 3: 14-16 to Revelation 6: 12-14). If Joel can be believed (and he can), that day will not be months and years but a single day. The Battle of Armageddon (Joel 3:2), will be fought following the 7 bowl judgments (Wrath of God) on the last day of the Great Tribulation. Joel continues his vision.

[30] ***And I will shew wonders in the heavens and in the earth,*** *blood, and fire, and pillars of smoke.*
[31] ***The sun shall be turned into darkness,*** *and the **moon into blood**, **before the great and the terrible Day of the LORD** come* Joel 2: 30-31

This should settle three key issues: (1) This exactly describes the same events which Christ prophesied and revealed as He broke the 6th seal in Revelation 6: 12-14. (2) The evidence is complete and overwhelming: The Day of the Lord is a single day on which Christ will descend from heaven and fight the Battle of Armageddon. Do not fail to recognize the significance of the next observation. (3) When the 6th Seal is removed by God; *every island and mountain will be moved out of its place*

(Revelation 6: 14). The things shown to John as the 6th seal is broken *coincide* with the pouring out of the *7th bowl* (Revelation 16: 17-20). Before Satan begins his reign of death and terror, he must first suffer defeat in a great war which will take place in the heavenlies between him and his fallen angels and Michael and his Holy Angels (Revelation 12:7). Satan will be cast out of heaven (Revelation 12: 8-9) and he will be furious with rage (Revelation 12:17). He will totally dominate and inherit the body of a slain European world leader and arise as the Antichrist (Revelation 13: 3-16). He will then break a peace treaty with Israel which has allowed them to build a new temple in Jerusalem (Revelation 11: 1-2). He will then sit in the Temple of God declaring Himself to be God. Isaiah called this broken Peace treaty a *Covenant of Death.*

Because ye have said: We have made a covenant with death, and with hell are we at agreement; when the overflowing scourge shall pass through, it shall not come unto us: for we have made lies our refuge, and under falsehood have we hid ourselves   Isaiah 28:15

Israel will be deceived and think that they are living in peace and safety. Suddenly, Satan as the Antichrist will turn upon Israel and annul the Covenant of Peace.

And your covenant with death shall be disannulled, and your agreement with hell shall not stand; when the overflowing scourge shall pass through, then ye shall be trodden down by it   Zachariah 28:18

Jesus Christ warned the Jews of this deception.

[**15**] *When ye therefore shall see the abomination of desolation, spoken of by Daniel the prophet, stand in the holy place, (whoso readeth, let him understand:)*
[**16**] *Then let them which be in Judaea flee into the* mountains
Matthew 24: 15-16

As soon as Satan is cast out of heaven, Satan will attack Jerusalem in what we have called the *Jerusalem Campaign* (Phillips, The Book of Revelation: *Mysteries Revealed*). He will pursue a fleeing remnant of Jews into the wilderness (Revelation 12: 14-15). Just as all hope seems to be lost, God will miraculously save these people with what appears to be a great earthquake (Revelation 12: 14-15). Satan as the Antichrist will be furious (Revelation 12:17a). He will then turn on all Jews and Christians (Revelation 12: 17b). During his 3.5 years reign of terror, he will kill 2/3 of all Jews (Zachariah 13: 8-9). In Zachariah Chapter 14, the Prophet jumps ahead 3.5 years and describes things which will happen just prior to the Battle of Armageddon…. which will take place at the Second Advent of Christ. If one will carefully read Zachariah 14: 1-12 there can be no doubt that when Christ returns to fight the Battle of Armageddon this is the Day of the Lord. It is also true that the Day of the Lord is exactly what we have said it is… *one day.*

But it shall be **one day** *which shall be known to the LORD, not day, nor night: but it shall come to pass, that at evening time it shall be light* Zachariah 14:7

Paul warned his Jewish brothers of this deception.

[1] *But of the times and the seasons, brethren, ye have no need that I write unto you.*
[2] *For yourselves know perfectly that the day of the Lord so cometh as a thief in the night.*
[3] *For when they shall say, Peace and safety; then sudden destruction cometh upon them, as travail upon a woman with child; and they shall not escape*   I Thessalonians 1-3

It is time to Review Revelation 6:14 and Revelation 16:20 to present the most compelling and convincing evidence that the 7 Seals only review events which are about to happen as the Great Tribulation begins.

As Christ removes the 6th seal, the following description of things to come are revealed to John.

And the heaven departed as a scroll when it is rolled together; and every mountain and island were moved out of their places.   Revelation 6:14

This exactly coincides with what will happen when the 7th Bowl is poured out upon all unbelievers.

And every island fled away, and the mountains were not found. Revelation 16:20

This is a specific, devastating event which will occur at only one moment in time. *Every* mountain and island will be moved and disappear. Such an event cannot be comprehended and even imagined. ***Are we to believe that these things will happen twice as necessitated by all Pre -Tribulation teachers?*** (3) The *Day of the Lord* is not a protracted period of time necessitated by a Pre-Tribulation theology or a Pre-Wrath theology but *one day*. Both Pre-Tribbers and Classical Pre-Wrath Rapture supporters *must* declare that the Day of the Lord is a period of time which spans both the 7 Trumpet and the 7 Bowl Judgments because Seal 6 reveals:

For the great day of his wrath is come; and who shall be able to stand? Revelation 6:17

Now, apply scriptural evidence and common sense to the Revelation Record. *Are we to believe that this incredible event will happen twice? ...Once when the 6th seal is broken* (Revelation 6:14) *and again at the end of the tribulation period when the 7th Bowl is poured out* (Revelation 16:20)? Such a conclusion cannot possibly be believed or sustained!!! The conclusion .... beyond any reasonable doubt....is that when the 6th seal is broken by Christ, John is shown what will happen just before Christ returns a 2nd time as King of Kings and Lord of Lords....not as a suffering servant but as a conquering King....Praise God Forever.

This universal misunderstanding is because all Pre-Tribulation and Classic Pre-Wrath Rapturists assume that the Seals, Bowls and Trumpets are all time delay events which occur in sequence. This demands a protracted period of time which is called the Wrath of God because of Revelation 6:17 which is part of the 6th Seal.

Finally note that a great earthquake will happen at that time, so great that such has never occurred since time began.

And I beheld when he had opened the sixth seal, and, lo, there was a **great earthquake***;* Revelation 6: 12a

This **great earthquake** was also predicted as the 6th seal is removed (Revelation 6:12). It will occur as the 7th and last bowl/vial is poured out (Revelation 16:18).

[**17**] *And the seventh angel poured out his vial into the air; and there came a great voice out of the temple of heaven, from the throne, saying:* ***It is done***.
[**18**] *And there were voices, and thunders, and lightnings; and there was a* **great earthquake***, such as was not since men were upon the earth, so mighty an earthquake, and so great*   Revelation 16: 17-18

We have shown convincing evidence that the 6 seals when broken by Christ are a preview of things to come, and will span either the entire last half of Daniel's 70th week (7 Years), or only the last 3.5 years of the Great Tribulation, depending upon whether the Great Tribulation is assumed to last. This depends upon *when* the Daniel 70 Week prophecy starts and how many days constitute a year (Phillips, The Daniel 70 Week Prophecy: *The Cornerstone of all Prophecy*). Within either assumption, the is believed to occur as the 7th Trumpet sounds on the *Jewish Feast of Trumpets*, which will occur just 10 days before the 2nd advent of Christ. We will show that this is the most likely scenario for the Rapture in Chapter 5.

The 7th and final seal is now broken and removed by Christ.

And when he had opened the seventh seal, there was silence in heaven about the space of half an hour
Revelation 8:1

The scroll which belonged to God can now be completely unrolled. It is written on both sides and contains a detailed description of end-time events. As Christ breaks the 7th seal, a sequence of events will be seen by John which are so incredible and devastating that heaven falls completely silent for about *half an hour*. We can only guess the actual earth-time duration of this period of time.

The contents of the 7 sealed scroll can now be revealed to John, who will write them for us in the last book of our holy Bible: The *Book of Revelation*. Thirty-five times in the Book of Revelation John said: *I saw*. John will actually *see* things which take place in the distant future (Revelation 1:19).

[2] *And **I saw** the seven angels which stood before God; and to them were given seven trumpets.*
[3] *And another angel came and stood at the altar, having a golden censer; and there was given unto him much incense, that he should offer it with the prayers of all saints upon the golden altar which was before the throne.*
[4] *And the smoke of the incense, which came with the prayers of the saints, ascended up before God out of the angel's hand.*
[5] *And the angel took the censer, and filled it with fire of the altar, and cast it into the earth: and there were voices, and thunders, and lightnings, and an earthquake.*
[6] *And the seven angels which had the seven trumpets prepared themselves to sound*   Revelation 8: 2-6

Revelation 8:2 implies that God Himself gives a trumpet to each of 7 mighty angels. Before the 7 trumpets can sound, another mighty angel appears with a *golden censor* which is filled with much incense. In remembrance of the *Altar of Incense* which stood before the *Holy of Holies* in the *Tabernacle* of Moses, which was only a copy of the true Altar of Incense that is before God's throne in heaven. A remarkable event is then shown to John. The incense is poured out of the golden censor and placed on the Altar of Incense. This mighty angel then takes the prayers of the saints and offers both up to God. *Where did these prayers come from?* They were identified when the scroll of truth was given to Jesus Christ to break the 7 seals and disclose its contents (Revelation 5: 6-8). What an astounding revelation! Evidently when a Christian prays to God, those prayers are recorded and kept by the 4 living beasts (zoa) and the 24 elders which stand before the throne of God. When this angel placed his incense upon the alter, the smoke of the burning incense and the prayers of the Saints ascended up to God. The next event is even more incredible and revealing. The angel takes the censor previously full of incense, and fills it with coals from the Golden Altar. He then casts these burning coals to the earth and there were voices, and thunders, and lightnings, and an earthquake.

This is exactly what happens 3. 5 years later as an angel pours out the 7th and final bowl upon the earth.

[**17**] *And the seventh angel poured out his vial into the air; and there came a great voice out of the temple of heaven, from the throne, saying: It is done.*
[**18**] *And there were voices, and thunders, and lightnings; and there was a great earthquake, such as was not since men were upon the earth, so mighty an earthquake, and so great*   Revelation 16: 17-18

Evidence Demands a Verdict

The scroll which was in the right hand of God and was given to Jesus Christ contains a record of the sequence of events which will terminate the Church Age. Jesus Christ will rapture out all who will accept Him as Lord and Savior; defeat Satan at the Battle of Armageddon after the 7

Bowl judgments are poured out upon an unbelieving world; initiate the 1000-year Millennial kingdom; and finally, usher in eternity. The scroll was sealed with 6 seals which when broken will predict and preview conditions (Seals 1-4) and events (Seals 5 and 6) which will take place during the next 3.5 years. The last half of Daniel's 70th week will begin when Satan is cast down to earth by Michael and the holy angels (Revelation 12: 7-8). The 7 trumpet judgments take place (Wrath of Satan), followed immediately by the 7 Bowl Judgments (Wrath of God). Note carefully that the 7 Trumpet Judgments (Wrath of God) cannot take place until Satan is cast out of heaven with 3.5 years to go in the Church Age. The last great event to take place is the *Battle of Armageddon.*

Once again…. the contents of the scroll cannot be known until all of the 7 seals are removed. As the Seals are broken by Christ, John is shown general conditions which will exist when the tribulation period begins (Seals 1-4); and several specific events which will occur (Seals 5 and 6). When Seal 7 is removed, Heaven stands in silence and awe because of the things which are about to take place. (2) The 7 Trumpets represent and describe the *Wrath of Satan* (Revelation 12:12) which is about to be unleashed upon the earth, and the 7 Bowls contain the *Wrath of God* (Revelation 15:1, Revelation 15:7 and Revelation 16:30) which will fall upon all unbelievers. Every Christian who is secure in Jesus Christ has been promised that they will not experience the *Wrath of God* (Romans 1:18, Romans 5:1, Colossians 3:6, I Thessalonians 1:10, I Thessalonians 5:9) …which is without controversy or ambiguity the 7 Bowl Judgments (Revelation 15:1, Revelation 15:7, Revelation 16:1).

The last 3.5 years of Daniels 70th week and the last 3.5 years of the Church Age are composed of two parts: (1) The 7 trumpet Judgments which are the *Wrath of Satan* and the 7 Bowl/Vial Judgments which are the *Wrath of God.* The entire period of Tribulation and Wrath is 1260 days. The Wrath of Satan (7 Trumpet Judgments) will fall upon all those who dwell upon the earth (believers and unbelievers) over a 1250-day time period and (2) The Wrath of God (7 Bowl Judgments) will fall upon all unbelievers over a 10-day period of time. A fundamental truth that is contained throughout the entire New Testament is that Christians will face suffering and affliction in this world and will have trials and tribulations. Jesus told us so:

Blessed are you when others revile you and persecute you and utter all kinds of evil against you falsely on my account. Rejoice and be glad, for your reward is great in heaven, for so they persecuted the prophets who were before you   Matthew 5: 11-12

John told us so:

In the world you will have tribulation. But take heart; I have overcome the world   John 16:33

Paul told us also:

Indeed, all who desire to live a godly life in Christ Jesus will be persecuted   II Timothy 3:12

We should not fear suffering and tribulation. While we may desire to be spared from suffering and tribulation in this life, we need to recognize that suffering is not antithetical to the Christian but rather part of the normal Christian life as we follow Christ in this world. All who have accepted Christ as their Lord and Savior will not be alive during the 3.5 years of great tribulation, but all will experience tribulation while on this earth. So, let us heed the call to the church in the Book of Revelation to hold fast to our faith in all circumstances. Jesus continually tells us that we should be ready because he will come at an hour we do not know and He will come quickly. Our lives could end at any time, so let us remain faithful and remind others of this important truth. As repeatedly stated, and revealed in the scriptures, those who believe upon Jesus Christ as the Son of God (Christians…Jew or Gentiles) will never experience the Wrath of God (Revelation 15:1, Revelation 15:7 and Revelation 16:1).

Those who accept and believe that Christ is the Son of God and become *Christians* will be rewarded with eternal life through Him. This is a free gift based upon faith and grace…but there was a great price that was paid for redemption from sin.

What is expected of any individual who has accepted Jesus Christ as their Lord and Savior?

Anyone who accepts Christ as their Lord and savior becomes part of the *Body of Christ*. Christ has risen, but every Christian is expected to proclaim the Gospel Message to unbelievers and to win souls to Christ. This is part of becoming a *new creature in Christ*. A fundamental and integral part of this mission is to convert the Jews to a blood-bought believer.

This is not just symbolic: Every born-again Christian represents Christ here on this earth: Preaching the Gospel of salvation and winning Souls to Christ. There are no exceptions…both Jew and Gentile believers. The Jews are God's chosen people, but they have been *blinded in part* until God removes the scales from their spiritual eyes. It is our responsibility and calling to win Jews to Christ. Make no mistake about it …Any Orthodox Jew (or anyone else) who does not believe in Jesus Christ as their Savior and Redeemer, and dies in a state of disbelief, will be tortured forever in the Lake of Burning Fire. This truth does not just apply to the Jews, but to Jews and Gentiles alike. I did not say this…Jesus did.

Jesus saith unto him, I am the way, the truth, and the life: no man cometh unto the Father, but by me
John 14:6

Neither is there salvation in any other: for there is none other name under heaven given among men, whereby we must be saved
Acts 4:12

A Pre-Tribulation Rapture in which all Christians are removed from earth is one of the worst lies ever placed by Satan upon theologians and ordinary Christians. The general belief and attitude of all Pre-Tribulation believers is that Christ will return some day (soon) and remove all Christians from the earth: *Just hang on. No Wrath will never be experienced by any Christian.* If this is true, who is left to preach the everlasting gospel, save souls, and transform unbelievers into true believers? If this is true: *When will anyone who accepts Christ during the Tribulation expect to get raptured and receive their rewards?* Many who would not be raptured out before the Tribulation begins might turn to Christ when they realize what has happened, but who will save them and tell them about Jesus Christ if every believer is gone? Those who would remain after a Pre-Tribulation rapture and turn to Christ as their Lord and Savior would have to go through *both* the Wrath of Satan and the Wrath of God, and possibly be Martyred for their faith. This division of Saints is not taught anywhere in scripture. *Is this really the plan of God?* My answer to that question is: *NO.* God has promised that *anyone* who accepts His Son as Lord and Savior and receives the free gift of eternal life *will not* experience the *Wrath of God.*

*Much more then, being now justified by his blood, we shall be saved from **wrath** through him* Romans 5:9

*For God hath not appointed us to **wrath**, but to obtain salvation by our Lord Jesus Christ* I Thessalonians 5:9

The obvious question for all readers should be: What is the *Wrath of God* that no Christian will experience? To answer this important question, the scriptures must be searched. Is any day or and period of time called the *Wrath of God....YES* and it is right where it should be! When the 7 Bowls of Gods Wrath are poured out in the Great Tribulation..

*And I saw another sign in heaven, great and marvelous, seven angels having the seven last plagues; for in them is filled up the **Wrath of God*** Revelation 15:1

*And one of the four beasts gave unto the seven angels seven golden vials full of the **Wrath of God**, who lives for ever and ever* Revelation 15:7

*And I heard a great voice out of the temple saying to the seven angels: Go your ways, and pour out the vials of the **Wrath of God** upon the earth* Revelation 16:1

It is convincing that if the Wrath of God are the 7 Bowl Judgments, the 6th Seal predicted not only that this will occur but when it will happen.

*For the **great day of his wrath is come**; and who shall be able to stand?*
Revelation 6:17

If all Christians are promised that they will never go through the Wrath of God, then obviously none will be on earth when the 7 Bowls are released upon all unbelievers. If every Christian is gone: *How and why did they escape?* We will show that they were all Raptured out at the 7th Trump.

Chapter 5

Rapture of the Saints

The Rapture Revealed

The Apostle Paul is our main source of information concerning the Rapture of all living saints, and the resurrection of all who have accepted Jesus Christ as their Lord and Savior. These include: (1) All who died in the Old Testament with the faith of Abraham that a redeemer would be sent by God to permanently forgive their sins. (2) All who would accept Jesus Christ (live or dead) as their redeemer under the New Covenant.

And the Redeemer shall come to Zion, and unto them that turn from transgression in Jacob, saith the LORD   Isaiah 59:20

Paul wrote that the redemption of all true believers would happen, but did not say when.

[**13**] *But I would not have you to be ignorant, brethren, concerning them which are asleep, that ye sorrow not, even as others which have no hope.*
[**14**] *For if we believe that Jesus died and rose again, even so them also which sleep in Jesus will God bring with him.*
[**15**] *For this we say unto you by the word of the Lord, that we which are alive and remain unto the coming of the Lord shall not prevent them which are asleep.*
[**16**] *For the Lord himself shall descend from heaven with a shout, with the voice of the archangel, and with the trump of God: and the dead in Christ shall rise first:*
[**17**] *Then we which are alive and remain shall be caught up together with them in the clouds, to meet the Lord in the air: and so shall we ever be with the Lord.*
[**18**] *Wherefore comfort one another with these words*
I Thessalonians 4: 13-18

The word *rapture* does not appear anywhere in the scriptures. In I Thessalonians 4:17 we are told that those saints which are alive or dead will be *caught up* to meet Christ in the air. The phrase *caught up* is translated from the Latin word *Raptura*, from which we derive the word *rapture*. There should be no ambiguity, because Jesus Christ told us *when* the Rapture would occur.

[**29**] *Immediately **after the tribulation of those days** shall the **sun be darkened**, and the **moon shall not give her light**, and the **stars shall fall from heaven**, and the powers of the heavens shall be shaken:*
[**30**] ***And then** shall appear the sign of the Son of man in heaven: and then shall all the tribes of the earth mourn, and **they shall see the Son of man coming in the clouds** of heaven with power and great glory.*
[**31**] *And he shall send his angels with a great **sound of a trumpet**, and **they shall gather together his elect** from the four winds, from one end of heaven to the other*　　　　　Matthew 24: 29-31

The *signs* of a Rapture were predicted to happen when the 6th seal is removed by Christ.

*And I beheld when he had opened the sixth seal, and, lo, there was a great earthquake; and the **sun became black** as sackcloth of hair, and the **moon became as blood***　　　　　Revelation 6:12

This event was predicted as the 6th Seal was removed, and in context it should take place late in the Tribulation period of time…and it does….as the 7th Trumpet sounds just before the *Wrath of God* (7 Bowl judgments) is unleashed upon all unbelievers. Every Christian will be gone… Raptured out as the 7th and last trump sounds. Everything falls into place if a Pre-Wrath Rapture takes place as the 7th Trumpet sounds.

Resurrection and Rapture

We have presented overwhelming evidence that the Seals only predict *conditions* (Seals 1-4), the martyrdom of Christians (Seal 5) and selected events (Seal 6) which are about to take place as the 7 Trumpets are sounded and the 7 Bowls are poured out. When Seal 7 is removed, there is silence in heaven. The scroll can be unrolled and the contents revealed. The 7 Trumpets are called the *Wrath of Satan* (Revelation 12:12) and the 7 Bowls are called the *Wrath of God* (Revelation 15:1, Revelation 15:7, Revelation 16:1). The 1st Day *of God's Wrath* is the first day after the church is Raptured, and the last day is the Battle of Armageddon (Isaiah 13:9, Isaiah 13:13, Zepeniah 1:15, Ezekiel 39:22, Zachariah 12:8). The Rapture will take place immediately after the 7th trumpet is blown on Tishri 1 (Jewish *Feast of Trumpets)* and the last day of God's Wrath will be Tishri 10 (Jewish *Feast of Yom Kippur*) which is also the Battle of Armageddon. Later in this Chapter, the 7 Feasts of Israel which provide a *blueprint* of end-time events will be discussed. For contrast and importance, the four mainstream rapture beliefs will now be briefly presented.

There are 4 main Rapture positions that are held by an overwhelming number of all theologians and Christians: (1) Pre-Tribulation Rapture (2) Mid-Tribulation Rapture (3) Post-Tribulation Rapture and (4) Classic Pre-Wrath Rapture.

1.0   Pre-Tribulation Rapture

A Pre–Tribulation rapture is held by most dispensationalists today, and is the most popular theology among prophecy teachers. It is a relatively new view that seems to have been popularized by a British pastor named John Nelson Darby around 1831 and by a Scottish girl named *Margaret McDonald* in early 1830. She had a *vision* and an *utterance* in a Presbyterian church pastored by Edward Irvin (1792-1834). John Darby, who was pastor of the *Church of Ireland*, accepted the vision as a divine prophecy from God and began to preach its acceptance. The fact that John Darby first popularized the pre-tribulation rapture doctrine around 1831 AD is unquestionably true. However, much credit must be given to C. I. Scofield. When Scofield wrote his popular *Scofield Reference Bible* in 1909, he was greatly influenced by Darby and adopted the belief of a Pre-Tribulation rapture. This concept never existed in the ancient church fathers and I can find no reference to a Pre-tribulation Rapture before 1800 AD. So, there you have it…. The *pre-tribulation Rapture* theory is only about 200 years old and places the rapture of the church *before* a commonly taught seven-year period of tribulation.

Authors Comment*: Another interesting observation concerning the pre-tribulation rapture position is that scriptural justification is largely based upon Revelation 4:1

After this I looked, and, behold, a door was opened in heaven: and the first voice which I heard was as it were of a trumpet talking with me; which said, come up hither, and I will show thee things which must be hereafter   Revelation 4:1

All Pre-Tribulation believers considerably stretch the imagination in asserting that when John was taken from the Island of Patmos in the spirit (Revelation 4:2), and transported to heaven, this represented the rapture of all saints. This cannot be true. *First*, when the rapture of all living Christians takes place, they will be taken to heaven by Jesus Christ Himself, who will meet them in the air. There is no hint that this took place in Revelation 4:1. *Second*, at the Rapture the righteous dead will be raised first. There is not even an indication that John was preceded by anyone dead. *Third*, those who are raptured out will be given a new, indestructible and non-corruptible body. There is not a single clue that John went through this type of transformation. *Fourth*, flesh and blood cannot enter into the kingdom of heaven (I Corinthians 15:50), so John was taken to heaven in the *spirit*. *Fifth*, when the rapture does take place, *all* of the saints (living and dead) will meet Christ in the air, and then they will forever be with the Lord. John returned to earth and lived several years after he penned the Book of Revelation. *Sixth,* When the saints are raptured, they will all be called forth by the sound of a *trumpet*. In Revelation 4:1 John was told to *come up here* by a *voice* which *sounded like a trumpet* (Revelation 1:10). *Seventh*, the only reason that John was taken to heaven was to see what *must take place hereafter* (Revelation 4:1). After being shown how the church age and the 1000-year Millennial Kingdom will end, John was told to return to Patmos and write the Book of Revelation. He lived for years after he was returned to earth.

The idea that John 4:1 types and represents the rapture is so far-fetched that it hardly deserves consideration, yet a pre-tribulation rapture is widely believed and taught in seminaries, bible study groups and in the pulpit.

2.0   Post-Tribulation Rapture

A Pre-Tribulation rapture was not taught or held by the ancient church fathers. The predominant position was that of a Post-Tribulation Rapture. This belief places the rapture of the church immediately *following* a 7-year period of tribulation, and after the 7 bowls have been poured out. The Rapture occurs just before the final Battle of Armageddon. The raptured saints then immediately return with Christ to join Him in the Battle. The post–tribulation belief has largely disappeared among modern prophecy teachers because of multiple scriptural problems which we will not address. A *Post-Tribulation* rapture position assumes that the church is not promised any protection from either the Wrath of Satan or the Wrath of God. In fact, there is no distinction between the two at all. The Post-Tribulation proponents teach that God's elect will have a full and clear understanding of the timing of the second coming of Christ, and Christ's coming will not catch believers by surprise…only those who are spiritually misinformed regarding the truth. Almost no modern prophecy teacher will propose a Post-Tribulation rapture.

3.0   Mid-Tribulation Rapture

The mid-tribulation rapture theory is exactly as the name indicates; it assumes that the rapture will occur just before Satan is cast down to earth in a great celestial battle (Revelation 12). The *ecclesia* who are raptured out are usually associated with the *Man-Child* in Revelation 12:5. The belief was spawned by (properly) recognizing that the Man-Child of Revelation 12 arc believers who will be raptured out at that time. One of the problems with this position is that the Man-Child would need to be composed of only living believers (Revelation 12: 1-4). Paul revealed that when the rapture will occur, those taken up to meet Christ in the air will be both living and dead… and there is not one hint that this is true in Revelation 12.

The Man-Child is immediately caught up to the throne as it is birthed. Another major problem is that if all believers are raptured out, how can Revelation 12:17 be explained? Almost all prophecy teachers assume that the Man-Child is Jesus Christ, But Revelation 12:5 clearly states that the Man-Child was birthed and immediately caught up to God. The mid-tribulation position has only a few supporters.

4.0 Classic Pre-Wrath Rapture

The most recent rapture theory to surface is called a *Pre- Wrath* rapture. It was popularized by Robert Van Kampen (*The Sign*) and Matthew Rosenthal (*The Pre-Wrath Rapture of the Church*). Rosenthal was a Jew who converted to Christianity. The classic Pre-Wrath Rapture position fails to distinguish between the *Wrath of Satan* and the *Wrath of God.* In a Pre-Wrath theology, the rapture takes place when the 6th seal is broken (Revelation 6:12). Like a Pre-Tribulation rapture, the Pre-Wrath Rapture does not deny but supports a 7-year tribulation period. *Exactly when* the Rapture occurs in the classic pre-wrath theology is a matter of choice, but it must take place as the 6th seal is removed. Van Kampen and Rosenthal both placed their entire belief in a Pre-Wrath rapture on the premise that Christians (the church) would be spared from *all* wrath (Revelation 6:17). This belief led him to believe that all wrath would commence as the 6th seal is removed because Revelation 6:17 clearly states that the *Day of His Wrath* has come. *First*, this would demand that *His Wrath* must mean *both* the Wrath of Satan and the Wrath of God, since the 7 Trumpet judgments and the 7 Bowl Judgments are yet to come. This also suggests that both the tribulation and wrath that will span the entire tribulation period must be attributed to God; which is simply untenable. It is true that the 7 Trumpet Judgments of Satan's Wrath are allowed by God, but this is hardly the same as being executed by God. *Second*, this demands that the *Day of Wrath,* which is mentioned in many Old and New Testament scriptures, cannot be a single day, but spans the 7 trumpet Judgments and the 7 Bowl Judgments.

The basic premise of both Van Kampen and Matthew Rosenthal is we believe, correct. Where both met an impasse in scriptural harmonization was/is a failure to recognize what we have presented as scriptural truth... that the seals simply provide an overview of the tribulation period and that all Christians are not spared from the Wrath of Satan but from the Wrath of God. Realizing this, all scriptural conflicts disappear between Revelation 6:17 and Revelation 16:1. Phillips has resolved all Classic Pre-Wrath difficulties and scriptural conflict by proposing a new Pre-Wrath Theory (Phillips, *A New Pre-Wrath Rapture Theory*).

The 7 Feasts of Israel

To understand Jewish Messianic expectations concerning Resurrection and Rapture, one must recognize and understand the meaning of the *7 Feasts of Israel*. They were ordained and established by God after He rescued the Children of Israel from Egyptian slavery (Leviticus 23). The 7 Feasts of Israel are historical in that they were to be observed forever as a memorial and remembrance of how God rescued them from Egyptian slavery, and then formed a New Nation which would by divine appointment serve the Lord and be the *apple of His eye.*

The 7 Festivals were called *moeds* whish mean *ordained* and *appointed* times, and each were to occur at a specific time each year. If the 7 festivals are to be held at specific time(s) during each year to recall and celebrate a past event (Exodus), why would Christians be interested? It is because that each feast is not only a *moed* but a *rehearsal*. A rehearsal of what? The 7 Feasts of Israel are not only *historical* but *prophetic* of things to come. They prophesy of the 1st and 2nd coming of our savior and redeemer…*Jesus Christ*. The first 4 Spring Feasts are (1) *The Feast of Pentecost* on Nisan 14 (2) The *Feast of Unleavened Bread* on Tishri 15-Tishri 21 (3) The *Feast of Firstfruits*, which is to be observed on the only Sunday that falls during the 7-day Feast of Unleavened Bread and the (4) *Feast of Pentecost*, which is held on the 50th day from the Feast of Firstfruits. Christ died on the Feast of Passover. He lay in the grave during the Feast of Unleavened Bread and satisfied the Feast of Firstfruits when he arose from the grave and ascended to His Father in Heaven. Fifty days after the Feast of Firstfruits (inclusive count), the Holy Spirit fell upon all of the people who were in Jerusalem on the Feast of Pentecost, just as Christ had promised and to satisfy parts of Joel (Matthew 3:11, Joel 2: 28-30).

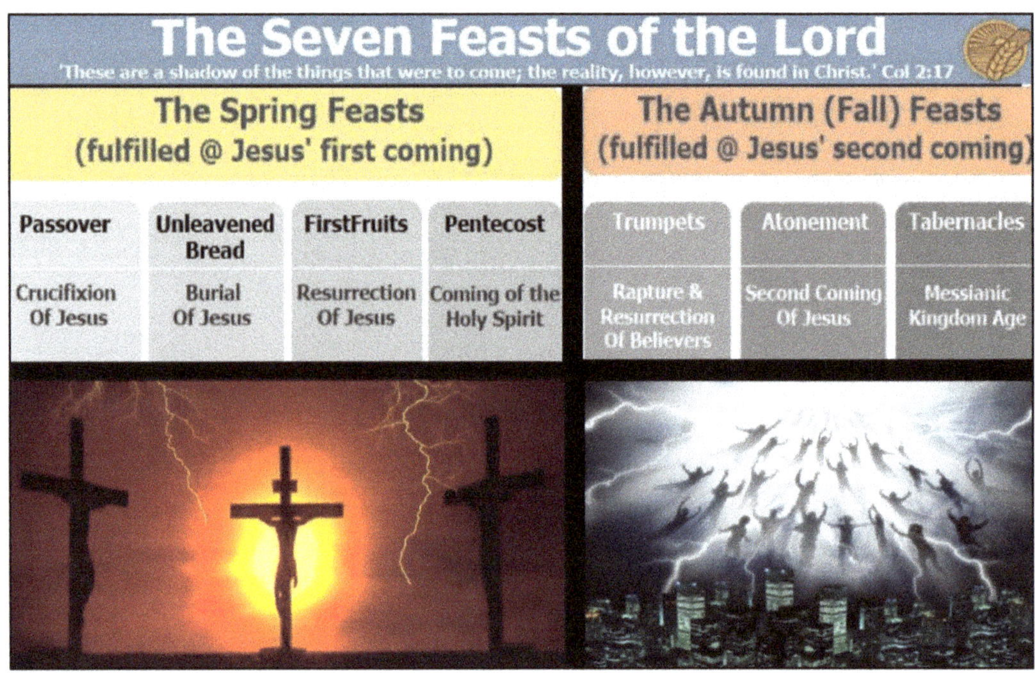

When Christ was crucified, ascended from the grave, rose to heaven, and sent the Holy Spirit on the *Day of Pentecost….* he completely and totally fulfilled the first 4 (Spring) Feasts of Israel. Christians who have studied the 7 Feasts of Israel realize that if the 1st four (Spring) Feasts of Israel spoke of the *first advent* of Christ, and that the last three (Fall) Feasts of Israel prophesy and speak of the *second coming* of Christ.

The Feast of Rosh Hashana (Feast of Trumpets) was to commemorate when the Law was given by God on Mt. Sinai; *The Feast of Yom Kippur* (Day of Atonement) is when each person is to confess their sins to God and seek to make things right with God. The *Feast of Tabernacles* (Sukkot) is the last of the 7 Holy convocations and it is to commemorate how the Children of Israel slept in tents during their 40 years of wandering in the Deserts of Sinai. Prophetically, the *Feast of Trumpets* is when the *Rapture* will take place; the *Battle of Armageddon* will take place on the *Feast of Yom Kippur* and the *Feast of Tabernacles* will usher in the 1000-year *Millennial Kingdom*.

The Feast of Trumpets also reminds us of the prophet Joel who prophesied of the end-times.

[1] *Blow ye the trumpet in Zion, and sound an alarm in my holy mountain: let all the inhabitants of the land tremble: for the **Day of the LORD** cometh, for it is nigh at hand;*
[2] *A day of darkness and of gloominess, a day of clouds and of thick darkness, as the morning spread upon the mountains: a great people and a strong; there hath not been ever the like, neither shall be any more after it, even to the years of many generations.*
[3] *A fire devourers before them; and behind them a flame burns: the land is as the garden of Eden before them, and behind them a desolate wilderness; yea, and nothing shall escape them.*
[4] *The appearance of them is as the appearance of horses; and as horsemen, so shall they run.*
[5] *Like the noise of chariots on the tops of mountains shall they leap, like the noise of a flame of fire that devours the stubble, as a strong people set in battle array.*
[6] *Before their face the people shall be much pained: all faces shall gather blackness.*
[7] *They shall run like mighty men; they shall climb the wall like men of war; and they shall march everyone on his ways, and they shall not break their ranks:*
[8] *Neither shall one thrust another; they shall walk everyone in his path: and when they fall upon the sword, they shall not be wounded.*
[9] *They shall run to and fro in the city; they shall run upon the wall, they shall climb up upon the houses; they shall enter in at the windows like a thief.*
[10] *The **earth shall quake** before them; the **heavens shall tremble**: the **sun and the moon shall be dark**, and the **stars shall withdraw their***

shining:

[11] *And the LORD shall utter his voice before his army: for his camp is very great: for he is strong that executes his word: for the **Day of the LORD** is great and very terrible; and who can abide it?*   Joel 2: 1-11

Joel is speaking of a *single* day, the day that Christ will return to fight the Battle of Armageddon. (Amos 5: 18-20; Zephaniah 1: 14-16; Isaiah 13: 9-10, 34: 4,8; Joel 2: 30-31, 3: 12-16; Revelation 6: 12-17). The second return of Jesus Christ to fight the Battle of Armageddon will be after a 10-day period of time between Tishri 1 and Tishri 10. These are called *Ten Days of Awe* by the Jews, and will end on the last day of the Age of Grace… the *Day of Atonement.* ***This period is considered the most holy time of the Jewish year.***

> For ten days, the Jewish people are to focus on their sins of the past year. As they contemplate how they have violated God's laws and injured other people, they are to confess their sins to God and seek to make things right with those they have violated. This is an important time of reflection and introspection to consider the consequence of their sins in order to be motivated not to repeat them. According to tradition, Rosh Hashanah is also called the Day of Judgment in which God opens up the Books of Life and Death for the year *https://www.forgivingforward.com*

The three Fall Feasts culminate on the *Feast of Tabernacles*: Tishri 15-Tishri 21). Tishri 21 is the 8th day of the Feast, and it is a day of joyous celebration. The Feast of Tabernacles will inaugurate the 1000-year millennial Kingdom, and Israel will finally inherit and live in the promised land.

It is widely believed that what we call the Rapture will occur on the *Feast of Trumpets* (Tishri 1). This is not the 2nd advent of Christ. The 2nd advent of Christ will be when He returns to earth to fight the Battle of Armageddon on the *Feast of Yom Kippur* (Tishri 10).

When God says *Go*…Jesus Christ will return to gather to Him those who believe upon Him (the ecclesia) at the sound of a trumpet…the last trumpet… and *meet them in the air.* The *Second Advent* of Christ is when he will physically return to Earth to fight the Battle of Armageddon. At this time, we are concerned with the *Rapture.*

Paul's Rapture Knowledge

The Apostle Paul provides the details of all scriptural truth concerning what we call the *Rapture.* The word *rapture* does not appear in the bible anywhere. It is taken from the Latin word *Raptura* which means to be *caught up* or *snatched away.* When the Latin Vulgate and the original Hebrew and Greek manuscripts were translated into Greek, the Greek word *Harpazo* was used which means to be *caught up* or *taken away.* When the KJV was translated from Greek... *Harpazo* was consistently translated as *caught up* (II Corinthians 12: 2-4, I Thessalonians 4:17, Revelation 12:5). In I Thessalonians 4: 14-17 Paul revealed:

[**15**] *For this we say unto you by the word of the Lord, that we which are alive and remain unto the **coming of the Lord** shall not prevent them which are asleep.*
[**16**] *For the Lord himself shall descend from heaven with a shout, with the voice of the archangel, and **with the trump of God**: and the dead in Christ shall rise first:*
[**17**] *Then we which are alive and remain shall be **caught up** together with them in the clouds, to meet the Lord in the air: and so shall we ever be with the Lord* I Thessalonians 4: 15-17

The Last Trump
Jesus also referred to the *rapture* in Matthew 24:31 as being launched by a *sound of a trumpet.* Paul later added that the rapture will be preceded by a *trumpet call of God* (I Thessalonians 4:16). In I Corinthians, he is specific about which trump.

[51] *Behold, I shew you a mystery; We shall not all sleep, but we shall all be changed,*
[52] *In a moment, in the twinkling of an eye, at the **last trump**: for the trumpet shall sound, and the dead shall be raised incorruptible, and we shall be* changed   I Corinthians 15: 51-52

Paul tells the saints to whom he is speaking (and us) that ***we will all be changed***, whether we are alive or dead, at the ***last trump***. Now that is fairly specific, but: *When would the **last trump** be sounded?* Those who casually read I Corinthians 15:52 are tempted to assume that since there are 7 trumpets which will be blown by angels in the Book of Revelation, and that the 7th trumpet is the last. Hence, one might conclude that the rapture will occur as the 7th trumpet sounds. This is certainly true, but it is not the real reason. The term ***last trump*** is a Jewish eschatological term always connected to the *Feast of Rosh Hashanah* or the *Feast of Trumpets*...which occurs in the 7th Jewish fall month on Tishri 1. Jewish people see Rosh Hashanah (Feast of Trumpets) as the beginning of a 10-day period of introspection, confession of sins and a time of repentance leading up to the *Feast of Yom Kippur (Day of Atonement)* on Tishri 10.

There are 30 days of blowing the trumpet on each day *preceding* Tishri A ***last trump*** is blown on the Feast of Trumpets. But there is also a trumpet blown on Tishri 10, so again…. *When is the last trumpet?* Here we must dig deeper into Jewish Rabbinical teachings. According to the ancient Jewish rabbis and teachers, the ***last trump*** is related to the ***binding of Isaac***. Recall that Abraham was called by God to sacrifice his only natural son Isaac, and he went up onto the mountain to do so. Ancient teachings say that Abraham went to where the ***Dome of the Rock*** now stands. He built an altar of sacrifice, and just as he was about to kill his son, God stayed his hand and produced a ***ram*** for a suitable sacrifice. This ram was offered as a ***burnt offerin***g to the Lord and totally consumed by fire. The only thing that survived was the two ram's horns. Tradition holds that the first horn was blown by God himself when the Law was given to Moses and the people at Mt. Sinai. The second horn…. The second and ***last horn***…. is to be blown at a future

Feast of Rosh Hashanah (Feast of Trumpets). The Feast of Trumpets is also called *Yom Teruah* or the *Day of Awakening Blast*. The *awakening blast* on some future Feast of Rosh Hashanah refers to a Jewish belief that the dead will be raised on this day. The resurrection of all Jews on Rosh Hashanah was widely taught and believed by the Jewish Rabbis of old and by the Jewish prophets.

The final, long, and most significant trumpet blast is called the ***last trump*** and will be sounded using the 2nd ram's horn. The fact that the last trump in the Book of Revelation is the last in a series of 7 does not fully justify that the Rapture of all living saints and the resurrection of all dead saints will occur when the 7th trumpet sounds, but supported by Jewish beliefs it is a distinct and logical possibility. The *Jewish* beliefs concerning the *last trump* are largely unknown to Western prophecy scholars who have not studied the *7 Feasts of Israel*.

Thy dead men shall live, together with my dead body shall they arise. Awake and sing, ye that dwell in dust: for thy dew is as the dew of herbs, and the earth shall cast out the dead   Isaiah 26:19

*For in the **time of trouble** he shall hide me in his pavilion: in the secret of his tabernacle shall he hide me; he shall set me up upon a rock*
Psalms 27:5

The *Time of Trouble (*Days of Awe*)* is the future 10-day period between Tishri 1 and Tishri 10 during which the 7 Bowls (Wrath of God) will be poured out upon an unbelieving world. Jewish belief is also that on the *last* Feast of Trumpets two Books will be opened (Daniel 7:10). These two books will be: (1) The *Book of Life* which contain the names of the righteous and (2) The *Book of Death* which contains the names of the wicked. It is also taught that there will be people who will not have their name inscribed in either book. Those people will be given 10 days to repent until their fate is sealed. These 10 days are between the Feast of Trumpets on Tishri 1 and the Feast of Yom Kippur on Tishri 10. This belief has been taught by Jewish Rabbis for thousands of years. The 10 days between the Feast of Trumpets (Tishri 1) and the Feast of Yom Kippur (Tishri 10) are called the *Days of Awe*. If a person turns to God, confesses his sins and offers a *Sin Offering* to God upon the *Altar of Sacrifice*...and if God accepts their offering for sins......they could be given another year to live. This was called *atonement* in the Old Testament which was only a *temporary covering* for sin (Hebrews 10:4).

On the Feast of *Yom Kippur* (Day of Atonement), the High Priest would cleanse himself, make a sin offering to God for himself and all of the people, walk behind the veil which separated the Ark of the Covenant from the Holy of Holies and the Holy Place, and plead with God to forgive the sins of the people. These rituals which were performed by the Jewish high priest have not been practiced since Herod's Temple fell in 70 AD. When Christ died on the Cross of Calvary, He became the final and perfect sacrifice for the sins of the world…He was the perfect sacrificial Lamb of God. Christ ended the ritual of this practice in 30 AD when He died on the Cross of Calvary. However, personal atonement for sin on Yom Kippur is *Jewish tradition* and is still taught and practiced today by individual Jews.

If this scenario causes one to reflect on the things which are written in this book...it should. We are currently in the *Church Age* or the *Times of the Gentiles*. In 30 AD Jesus Christ...who is our eternal high priest.... died on the Cross of Calvary and offered himself as the permanent, final, and perfect sacrifice for all sins (past and present). Since that point in time, the rituals and atonement (temporary covering) for sins that were practiced in the Old Testament are meaningless. The entire sacrificial system and the rituals which took place year after year on the 7 Holy Feasts of Israel are finished. However, there will be a future *Day of Yom Kippur* on which all of Israel will turn to Jesus Christ and be saved. It is the eternal plan of God that Israel will be blinded in part during this Church Age (there will be a believing remnant of Jews during the Church age), and there will be a future 10-day period of repentance (Tishri 1 - Tishri 10) during which all of Israel will be saved…those who are alive and remain.   It should now be clear that the end-times theology proposed in this book are perfectly in line with Jewish expectations…Which they must be.

The average Christian does not take the time to research biblical principles and try to resolve scriptural difficulties by studying Jewish beliefs. Remember that each of the 7 Feasts of Israel is a *remembrance* of what God did when He rescued them from Egyptian slavery, but they also *prophesy* of His 1st and 2nd coming. The First 4 Feasts are all in the Spring, and each was exactly satisfied in the 1st advent of Jesus Christ. The last 3 feasts are in the Fall, and they teach of His 2nd advent. There was a trumpet blown on each of the 7 Feasts of Israel, and there will be a Jewish *last trump* blown on the *last Feast of Trumpets*. Paul clearly taught that there would be a trumpet that would be blown to initiate the rapture, and that it would be the *last trump*. Is there a connection?

The Olivet Discourse
Once again, notice again what Christ says in the ***Olivet Discourse.***

[**29**] *Immediately **after** the tribulation of those days shall the sun be darkened, and the moon shall not give her light, and the stars shall fall from heaven, and the powers of the heavens shall be shaken:*
[**30**] *And **then** shall appear the sign of the Son of man in heaven: and then shall all the tribes of the earth mourn, and **they shall see the Son of man coming in the clouds** of heaven with power and great glory.*
[**31**] *And he shall send his angels with a great **sound of a trumpet**, and they shall **gather together his elect** from the four winds, from one end of heaven to the other*   Matthew 24: 29-31

Notice several extremely important *clues* in this discourse.

- This is clearly the ***rapture*** of the church revealed by Paul.
- It occurs ***after*** the tribulation of those days (not before, not in the middle).

- The sun is darkened, moon loses her light, and the heavens are disturbed. These are events which occur **after the 7th trumpet is sounded** (Joel 3: 15-16, Revelation 11:19).
- Everyone will see this happening… and it will be a **sign.**
- He (Christ) will send his angels to **gather the elect to him**.

The conclusion is that the rapture occurs immediately after what Christ called a great tribulation period at the **sound of a trumpet**. This perfectly aligns with Revelation 11: 15-19, ancient Jewish beliefs, and the prophetic meaning of the 7 Feasts of Israel. The 7 bowl judgments will be poured out upon all *unbelievers* over a 10-day period of time between the Feast of Trumpets and the Feast of Yom Kippur. This is the *Wrath of God* upon a non-believing world. *Why does the rapture occur before the 1ˢᵗ bowl is poured out?* Listen carefully, understand and open your mind…Christ answered this question also

*For then shall be **great tribulation, such as was not since the beginning of the world** to this time, no, nor ever shall be*   Matthew 24:21

*Much more then, being now justified by his blood, **we shall be saved from wrath** through him*   Romans 5:9

Christ warned us that there would be Great Tribulation that would one day fall upon all who are on the earth. However, there is a difference in experiencing *tribulation* and the *Wrath of God.* the proper way to determine what the Wrath of God actually involves is to look for other verses in the Holy Scriptures which define what it is. There is no question that the Wrath of God in the Tribulation Period are the 7 Bowl Judgments (Revelation 15:1, Revelation 15:7 and Revelation 16:1). Clearly, if the Rapture of all living saints occurs as the 7ᵗʰ trumpets sound no born-again Christian will experience the Wrath of God. Note that some would argue that those who might be raptured in either a Pre-Tribulation Rapture, a Mid-Tribulation Rapture or a classic Pre-Wrath Rapture will ever go through the 7 Bowl Judgments. This is obviously true, but in any case, those who are saved between the Rapture and the

Battle of Armageddon will have to go through God's Wrath…. And this is contrary to what has been promised to all true-believers. *Is there any doubt that Christ is prophesying of the 7 Bowl Judgments which are the Wrath of God (Revelation 15:1, Revelation 16:1)?*

Christ warned us that we would experience great tribulation in the end-times, but we are assured that no one who has believed upon His holy name before the rapture occurs at the 7th Trumpet will ever experience the *Wrath of God.*

[21] *For then shall be great tribulation, such as was not since the beginning of the world to this time, no, nor ever shall be*

 [22] *And except those days should be shortened, there should no flesh be saved: but for the elect's sake those days shall be shortened.* Matthew 24:22

After the Rapture occurs, there will be *great tribulation.* He stated that this tribulation would be worse than anything before it, and so bad that such severity would never occur again. The 7 Bowl judgments follow the 7 Trumpet Judgments and by reading Revelation 16: 1-21 it should be obvious that nothing which has previously occurred can compare to the Wrath and Tribulation that will take place as the 7 Bowls are poured out upon the earth. We have previously confirmed by scripture that the elect of God would not go through this wrath. The only reasonable conclusion is that the Rapture of all saints will occur as a Trumpet sounds (not at a voice that *sounds* like trumpet …... Revelation 4:1), and it will take place *after* Satan unleashes Great Tribulation (Wrath of Satan) upon all who refuse to worship him as God, but *before* the Wrath of God falls upon all unbelievers. Christ himself revealed this to his apostles in the Olivet Discourse and over 2000 years earlier by the prophet Joel.

[29] *Immediately **after the tribulation of those days** shall the sun be darkened, and the moon shall not give her light, and the stars shall fall from heaven, and the powers of the heavens shall be shaken:*

[30] *And **then shall appear the sign of the Son of man in heaven**: and then shall all the tribes of the earth mourn, and **they shall see the Son of man coming** in the clouds of heaven with power and great glory.*
[31] *And he shall send his angels with a great sound of a trumpet, and they shall gather together his elect from the four winds, from one end of heaven to the other*   Matthew 24: 29-31

Joel confirmed these words of Christ over 500 years earlier.

[30] *And I will shew wonders in the heavens and in the earth, blood, and fire, and pillars of smoke.*
[31] *The sun shall be turned into darkness, and the moon into blood, before the great and the terrible day of the LORD come.*
[32] *And it shall come to pass, that **whosoever shall call on the name of the LORD shall be delivered**: for in mount Zion and in Jerusalem shall be deliverance, as the LORD hath said, and in the remnant whom the LORD shall call*   Joel 2: 28-32

 Paul was a 3rd witness to this great event.

[16] *For the **Lord himself shall descend from heaven with a shout**, with the voice of the archangel, and **with the trump of God**: and the dead in Christ shall rise first:*
[17] *Then we which are alive and remain shall be **caught up** together with them in the clouds, to meet the Lord in the air: and so shall we ever be with the Lord.*
[18] *Wherefore comfort one another with these words*   I Thessalonians 4: 13-18

Paul revealed that Christ would *descend from heaven…* and with the *sound of a trumpet* all believers… living or dead…will be called to meet him in the air where they will be with Him forever. In his first letter to the Church at Corinth, Paul revealed more about the call of a trumpet.

[51] *Behold, I shew you a **mystery**; We shall not all sleep, but **we shall all be changed**,*
[52] *In a moment, in the twinkling of an eye, **at the last trump**: for the*

trumpet shall sound, and the dead shall be raised incorruptible, and we shall be changed   I Corinthians 15:52

Christ will call forth His ecclesia… living and dead…. to meet Him in the air at the sound of a trumpet…the *Last Trumpet*. Many have misunderstood the phrase *at the last trumpet*, and have assumed that since there is a series of 7 trumpets blown during the Tribulation period the 7th trumpet is the last in a series of 7 and that is when the Rapture will occur. That is true, but that is not what Paul meant when he said at the *last trump*. Paul was a Jew who by his own admission was a Pharisee, the son of a Pharisee (Acts 23:26), and educated by the most respected teacher of his time: *Gamaliel*. The last trump is an eschatological term which is part of Jewish beliefs and Rabbinical teaching.

Summary and Conclusions

This chapter has examined when the *Day of the Lord* (Rapture) will take place. The rapture of all living believers and the resurrection of all the righteous dead is not a Pre-Tribulation Rapture, but a Pre-Wrath Rapture. It is not the traditional Pre-Wrath Rapture popularized by Rosenthal, Van-Kampen, and a host of other Pre-wrath believers… but a rapture which: (1) Recognizes that the 7 Seal Judgments cannot be serial with both the 7 Trumpet Judgments or the 7 Bowl Judgments. (2) Recognizes that there is a critical biblical distinction between *Tribulation* and *Wrath*. Specifically, what we have called the *Wrath of Satan* (7 Trumpet Judgments) is *Tribulation,* and the *Wrath of God* (7 Bowl Judgments) is severe and devastating Wrath. (3) Recognizes that every Born-Again Christian will never experience the Wrath of God and (4) identifies the **Day of Jesus Christ** with the **Rapture** of the Saints and the **Day of the Lord** with **both** the Battle of Armageddon and the Day of God's Wrath at the end of the 1000-year Millennial Kingdom when He will personally remove all sin from the earth, and then renovate the earth by fire. All three will be single day events.

A great deal of evidence has been presented to support that the Rapture will occur as the 7th trumpet (shofar) is blown. Is has also been discussed and shown that the expectations of traditional Jews and their core beliefs concerning the resurrection of righteous Jews support both the beliefs and conclusions of this book…... Actually, it could be no other way.

For by one Spirit are we all baptized into one body, whether we be Jews or Gentiles, whether we be bond or free; and have been all made to drink into one Spirit   I Corinthians 12:13

It is God's eternal plan that not only the Gentiles, but His chosen people…Israel…will turn from their current disbelief and be saved… but not until the fullness of the Gentiles has come to pass. This will happen as the Church age draws to a close

Brethren, my heart's desire and prayer to God for Israel is, that they might be saved.   Romans 10:1

[25] For I would not, brethren, that ye should be ignorant of this mystery, lest ye should be wise in your own conceits; that blindness in part is happened to Israel, until the fulness of the Gentiles be come in. [26] And so all Israel shall be saved: as it is written: There shall come out of Sion the Deliverer, and shall turn away ungodliness from Jacob: [27] For this is my covenant unto them, when I shall take away their sins Romans 11: 25-27

And the Redeemer shall come to Zion, and unto them that turn from transgression in Jacob, saith the LORD. And the Redeemer shall come to Zion, and unto them that turn from transgression in Jacob, saith the LORD   Isaiah 59:20

Who would not want to be a part of this transformation of Israel and every other person on earth? If all of Israel (those who remain alive) will be saved, the church will play a major role. Oh, what a glorious time… thousands and perhaps millions of Jews and Gentiles will finally realize that their only hope of salvation is Jesus Christ. This is a time when Christians will preach the gospel and save many souls from eternal damnation. *Who would not want to be there?*

Chapter 6

Parables and the Tribulation Timeline

The key to understanding the timeline in the Book of Revelation is to understand what Jesus Christ said concerning when He would return again and the signs that would herald His second coming (Luke 5:1-3, Mark 4:1, and Matthew 13:1–3). Jesus had been teaching and healing near His home in Capernaum. One day He was teaching on the Bank of the Dead Sea, and people began to gather in large numbers to hear the Master. Pressed by the crowd, He found a boat and rowed a short distance from the shore to speak to the crowd. On this occasion Christ began to teach through a series of Parables: He taught the *Parable of the Sower* (Matthew 13: 18-23), The *Parable of The Leaven* (Matthew 13: 33), The *Parable of a Treasure Found in a Field* (Revelation 13:44), The *Parable of the Pearl of Great Price* (Revelation 13: 45-46, The *Parable of the Fishing Net* (Revelation 13: 47-50) and The *Parable of The Wheat and Tares* (Matthew 13: 24-30). Upon finishing His teaching, Jesus retired with His disciples and His apostles to His house in Capernaum. The disciples and apostles must have been confused by the words of Jesus, because one of the disciples asked Jesus: "Will you explain the Parable of the Wheat and Tares"? (Matthew 13:36).

[24] *Another parable put He forth unto them, saying: The kingdom of heaven is likened unto a man which sowed good seed in his field:*
[25] *But while men slept, his enemy came and sowed tares among the wheat, and went his way.*
[26] *But when the blade was sprung up, and brought forth fruit, then appeared the tares also.*
[27] *So the servants of the householder came and said unto him, Sir, didst not thou sow good seed in thy field? from where did the tares*

spring up??

[28] *He said unto them, An enemy hath done this. The servants said unto him: Should we go and gather them up?*

[29] *But he said, Nay; lest while ye gather up the tares, ye root up also the wheat with them.*

[30] *Let both grow together until the harvest: and in the time of harvest I will say to the reapers, Gather ye together first the tares, and bind them in bundles to burn them: but gather the wheat into my barn*
Matthew 13: 24-30

In an act of patience and understanding, Jesus began to explain the Parable.

- The *field* is the world
- Jesus Christ was the *sower* of the Good Seed (Wheat)
- The *Good seed* are the Children of the Kingdom
- Satan was the Sower of the *Bad seed* (Tares)
- The Bad seed are the *Children of Satan*
- The *Reapers* are Angels
- The Time of *Harvest* is at the *Rapture* for the *wheat* and the *Battle of Armageddon* for the *Tares*
- The *Tares* will be gathered by the angels and Burned in the Fire

The enemy (Satan) had come and sown the seeds of Tares with the good seeds of Wheat. Tares are a type of weed that is found with wheat. If you have ever seen a wheat field in the early stages of growth, one cannot tell the difference between the wheat and tares. As the field matures (before the grain shoots forth from the stalk), the tares are higher than the wheat and after maturity can be easily seen. The botanical name for tares is *Lolium temulentum* and it is commonly known as *darnel*. Some people call it *false wheat* because it looks so similar to wheat in appearance and even belongs to the same family of cereals. It has no nutritional relevance for humans. It is classified as weeds, an unwanted plant. This may seem to be a trivial fact, but it is critical to understanding the rest of the Parable. *The Tares cannot be distinguished from the wheat until just before the harvest.*

In the Parable the servants had become aware of the Tares, and they approached the landowner with a plan: *Should we go into the field and pull the Tares from among the wheat?* The land owner (Jesus Christ) responded: *NO….* If you pulled the Tares up out of the field, it might uproot the precious wheat also. ***Let them grow together until the harvest***, and I will tell the reapers (Holy angels) at the harvest to gather them into bundles to burn them later and take the precious wheat to my barn (heaven). Here we should note that there is the field, the barn and the house. The barn is always between the field and the house. Remember this later. Jesus is teaching us that our job as Christians is to preach the gospel message to all that will listen, and do not harshly judge those who we might feel are hopeless sinners. Our job is to plant the good seed, not to judge. Jesus said: *Allow them both to grow together, and I will judge.* A critical question is: *When will the Wheat be separated from the Tares?* Christ said…... *Let them both grow and exist together **until the harvest**, and that that time **I will instruct the angels** to bundle up the Tares and gather the precious wheat into my barn.*

When is the ***harvest***? It has previously been determined in Chapter 2 that the harvest is the Rapture which will take place on the *Day of the Lord*. This has been determined by examining information from both the Old and New Testament. If this conclusion is correct, we should be able to confirm it from the Book of Revelation……. *And we can.*
In Revelation Chapter 14 we find:

[**14**] *And I looked, and behold a white cloud, and upon the cloud one sat like unto the Son of man, having on his head a golden crown, and in his hand a sharp sickle.*

[**15**] *And another angel came out of the temple, crying with a loud voice to him that sat on the cloud, Thrust in thy sickle, and reap: for the time is come for thee to reap; for the harvest of the earth is ripe.*

[**16**] *And he that sat on the cloud thrust in his sickle on the earth; and the earth was reaped.*

[**17**] *And another angel came out of the temple which is in heaven, he also having a sharp sickle.*

[**18**] *And another angel came out from the altar, which had power over fire; and cried with a loud cry to him that had the sharp sickle, saying, Thrust in thy sharp sickle, and gather the clusters of the vine of the earth; for her grapes are fully ripe.*

[**19**] *And the angel thrust in his sickle into the earth, and gathered the vine of the earth, and cast it into the great winepress of the wrath of God*
Revelation 14: 14-19

Even a casual examination and comparison of Revelation 14: 14-19 to Matthew 13: 24-30 will confirm that they are referring to exactly the same thing. Both can also be compared to Matthew 24: 29-31 and Revelation 11: 15-18.

[**29**] *Immediately **after the tribulation of those days** shall the **sun be darkened, and the moon shall not give her light, and the stars shall fall from heaven, and the powers of the heavens shall be shaken:***
[**30**] *And then shall appear the **sign of the Son of man in heaven**: and then shall all the tribes of the earth mourn, and they shall see the Son of man coming in the clouds of heaven with power and great glory.*
[**31**] ***And he shall send his angels** with a great sound of a trumpet, and*

they shall gather together his elect from the four winds, from one end of heaven to the other   Matthew 24: 29-31

[**15**] *And the seventh angel sounded; and there were great voices in heaven, saying,* **The kingdoms of this world are become the kingdoms of our Lord, and of his Christ**; *and he shall reign for ever and ever.*
[**16**] *And the four and twenty elders, which sat before God on their seats, fell upon their faces, and worshipped God,*
[**17**] *Saying, We give thee thanks, O Lord God Almighty, which art, and wast, and art to come; because thou hast taken to thee thy great power, and hast reigned.*
[**18**] *And the nations were angry, and* **thy wrath is come**, *and the* **time of the dead, that they should be judged, and that thou shouldest give reward unto thy servants the prophets, and to the saints, and them that fear thy name, small and great**; *and shouldest destroy them which destroy the earth*   Revelation 11: 15-18

It is now possible to determine the following beyond any reasonable doubt.

- The *Day of Jesus Christ* is the *Rapture* of the saints
- The rapture corresponds to the separation of the wheat from the tares *after the tribulation* of those days.

   Authors Comment: The phrase *after the tribulation* (Matthew 24:29) does not necessarily imply that the Rapture will be after the entire tribulation has run its course. In fact, Jesus Christ made the following comments:

And this gospel of the kingdom shall be preached in all the world for a witness unto all nations; and then shall the end come   Matt. 24:14

[**21**] *For then shall be great tribulation, such as was not since the beginning of the world to this time, no, nor ever shall be.*

[22] *And except those days should be shortened, there should no flesh be saved: but for the elect's sake those days shall be shortened*
    Matt. 24: 21-22

> ***Authors Comment:*** *Jesus Christ said that: the end would not come until the gospel message is preached throughout the entire world.* After His resurrection and ascension, Christ told His disciples (by extension His body called the church also) to go throughout the world and preach the Gospel. This is called the *Great Commission*. This has been a command of Jesus Christ for almost 2000 years now. Is it possible that ordinary Christians can fulfill this commission, even to places in the darkest reaches of the Congo or Brazil?......Not likely. This command is still to the Body of Christ to do all we can, but this is not what Christ was referring to. The fulfilment of this command will be by angels in Revelation 14:6.

And I saw another angel fly in the midst of heaven, having the everlasting gospel to preach unto them that dwell on the earth, and to every nation, and kindred, and tongue, and people   Revelation 14:6

The *Great Tribulation* in Matthew 24:21 is the 10 Days between the Jewish calendar dates of Tishri 1 (Rapture) - Tishri 10 (Battle of Armageddon) which is the *Wrath of God* (7 Bowl Judgments). All saints will be raptured from the earth before this 10-day period…... not one born-again Christian will be left. This is *exactly* what Jesus Christ told His disciples (and us): *except those days should be shortened, there should no flesh be saved: but for the elect's sake those days shall be shortened* (Revelation 24:22). Note that the entire period of the Great Tribulation will not be cut short for the elect, but only the last 10-days. The following biblical truths should now be clear.

- The gospel which will be preached throughout the world is recorded in Revelation 14:6 just before the Rapture occurs in Revelation 14: 14-16
- The Rapture will take place as the 7th Trumpet sounds (Revelation 11: 15-19)
- Every living, born-again Christian will be raptured out at the 7th Trumpet because no Saint will ever experience the *Wrath of God* (Romans 1:18, Colossians 3:6, I Thessalonians 1:10, I Thessalonians 5:9) which are the *7 Bowls of God's Wrath* (Revelation 15:1, Revelation 16:1)

Chapter 7
Mysteries Resolved

The purpose of this book is to use scriptural clues, Jewish Messianic expectations and the Words of Jesus Christ to establish beyond reasonable doubt that the following results are truth.

- The *Day of Jesus Christ* is the day when Christ our Lord and Savior will return to *Rapture* all Born-Again believers and *resurrect* all who have died in faith that Christ was their redeemer. The Rapture will be on a single day: Tishri 1: *The Feast of Trumpets*
- The *Day of the Lord* is the day when Christ will return to fight the *Battle of Armageddon*. It will be on a single day: Tishri 10: *The Feast of Yom Kippur*
- The *Rapture* on Tishri 1 (Feast of Trumpets) and the *Battle of Armageddon* will be bracketed by a 10-day period of time called the Jewish *Days of Awe* which will end the Church age on Tishri 10. This period of time is when the *Wrath of God* (7 Bowl Judgments) will be poured out upon all unbelievers.
- There is a *second Day of the Lord* which has been overlooked by most if not all Prophecy teachers (II Peter 3:6-12). It will be on the last day of the 1000-Year Millennial Kingdom (Revelation 20: 7-9). It will be a *single day* on which God Himself will finally destroy Satan and *all* unbelievers. This will immediately be followed by the *Great White Throne Judgment* and the renovation of the earth by fire. After all sin is removed from the earth, and the earth has been purified.... eternity will begin and we will *Forever be with the Lord.*

The following diagram graphically depicts these end-time events.

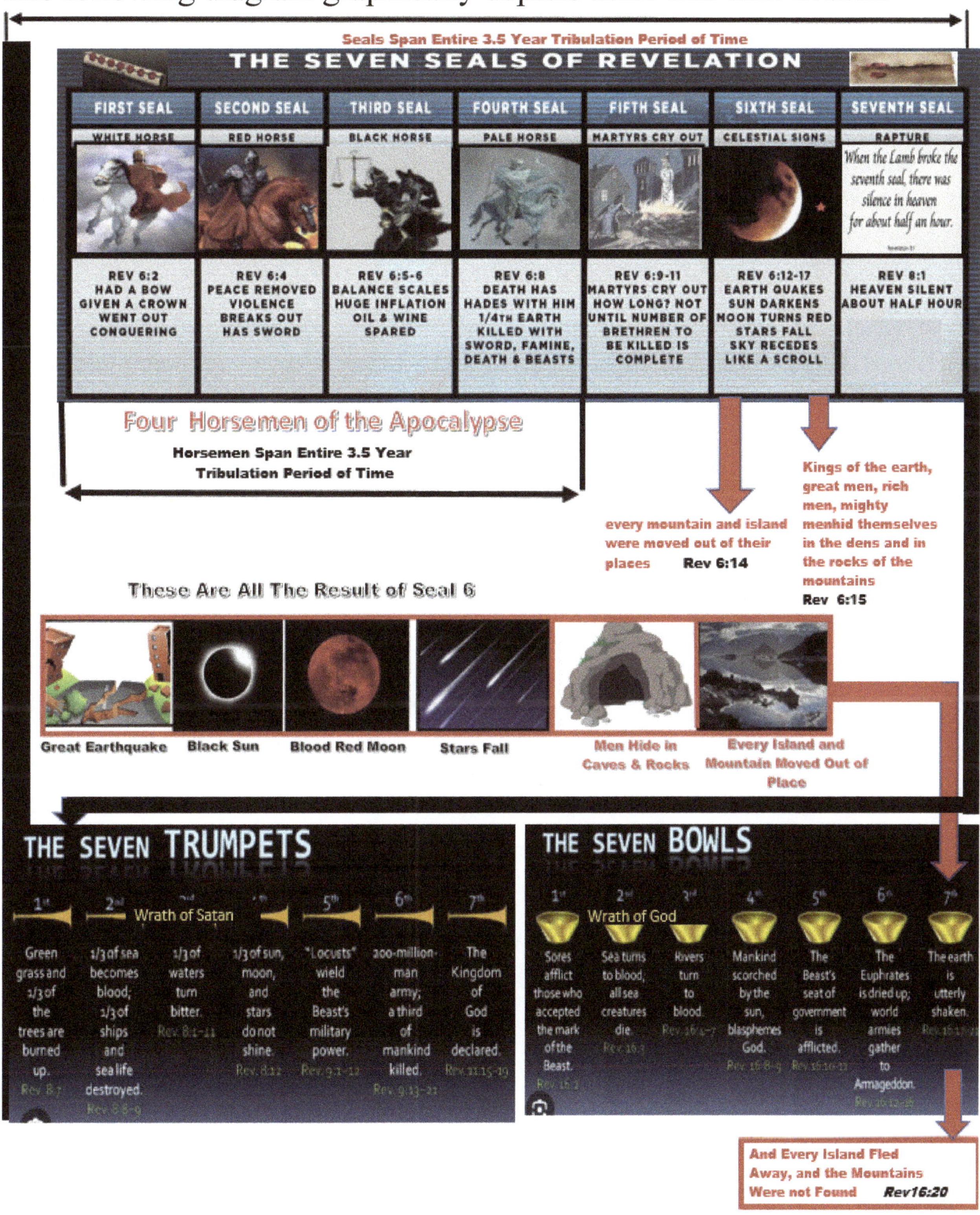

The 6 Seals must be removed by Jesus Christ before the contents of the large scroll can be revealed to the Apostle John. The 6 Seals do not

represent any time-delay events when they are removed, and they are not in a sequential lock-step relationship with the 7 Trumpet Judgments and the 7 Bowl/Vial judgments They predict 5 general conditions and one set of specific events which will take place when the Great Tribulation begins. The **Wrath** *of the Tribulation* cannot begin until Satan is cast down to earth and banned from the 2nd and 3rd heaven. He will be furious and wage war against all Jews and Christians. Note that when the 6th seal is removed, there is a prediction that there will be a *great earthquake,* the *sun will turn black,* the *moon will turn blood red* and there will be *cosmic disturbances.* Can we confirm that these signs will all be seen at the end of the age just before the Battle of Armageddon? *Yes.* Jesus Christ made the following statement.

[**29**] *Immediately **after the tribulation** of those days shall the **sun be darkened**, and the **moon shall not give her light**, and the **stars shall fall from heaven**, and the powers of the **heavens shall be shaken**:*
[**30**] *And then shall appear the **sign** of the Son of man in heaven: and then shall all the tribes of the earth mourn, and they shall see the Son of man coming in the clouds of heaven with power and great glory.*
[**31**] *And he shall send his angels with a great **sound of a trumpet**, and they shall gather together his elect from the four winds, from one end of heaven to the other*   Matthew 24: 29-31

There can be little doubt that Jesus Christ is speaking of the *Day of Jesus Christ* which is the *Rapture* of the saints. This is late in the tribulation (at the 7th Trump), which is just where it should be since the 6th Seal is predicting something which will happen late in the Tribulation after the first 5 Seals are removed. (The 7th Seal is a period of silence in preparation for the Great Tribulation to begin). It is possible that this period of silence could be when Satan and his unholy angels battle Michael and his holy angels (This is only a possibility and cannot be proved from scripture).

Revelation 6:14 compared to Revelation 16:20 is *proof* that the 6 Seals are not sequenced with the 7 Bowls and 7 Trumpets, but only preview and predict things to come.

And the heaven departed as a scroll when it is rolled together; and every mountain and island were moved out of their places   Revelation 6:14

And every island fled away, and the mountains were not found
Revelation 16:20

Revelation 6:14 is a description of what is predicted by the removal of Seal 6, and Revelation 16:20 is the fulfillment of Revelation 6:14 when Bowl 7 is poured out upon all unbelievers. It is *inconceivable* that such a specific, supernatural event could take place two times in the Great Tribulation.

Note that Revelation 6:17 is perfectly consistent with when the *Wrath of God* will take place. The Wrath of God are the 7 Bowl Judgments (Revelation 15:1, Revelation 16:7 and Revelation 16:1) which follow the 7 Trumpet Judgments. We have proposed that the 7th and final trumpet is the *Rapture* of the saints. If we examine what will happen when the 7th Trumpet Judgment takes place near certainty becomes certainty.

[**15**] *And the **seventh angel sounded**; and there were great voices in heaven, saying, **The kingdoms of this world are become the kingdoms of our Lord**, and of his Christ; and he shall reign for ever and ever.*
[**16**] *And the four and twenty elders, which sat before God on their seats, fell upon their faces, and worshipped God,*
[**17**] *Saying, We give thee thanks, O Lord God Almighty, which art, and wast, and art to come; because thou hast taken to thee thy great power, and hast reigned.*
[**18**] ***And the nations were angry, and thy wrath is come,** and the **time of the dead, that they should be judged, and that thou shouldest give reward unto thy servants the prophets, and to the saints**, and them that*

fear thy name, small and great; and shouldest destroy them which destroy the earth   Revelation 11: 15-18

If anyone is honest, removes all previous bias, and reads Revelation 11: 15-18…… it is inconceivable that a 7th Trump Rapture would not be accepted as biblical truth.

The signs that will signal the end is very near will happen when Bowls 5-7 are poured out upon all unbelievers

[**10**] *And the fifth angel poured out his vial upon the seat of the beast; and his **kingdom was full of darkness**   Revelation 16:10*

[**16**] *And he gathered them together into a place called in the Hebrew tongue **Armageddon**.*
[**17**] *And the seventh angel poured out his vial into the air; and there came a great voice out of the temple of heaven, from the throne, saying, **It is done**.*
[**18**] *And there were voices, and **thunders, and lightnings**; and there was a **great earthquake**, such as was not since men were upon the earth, so mighty an earthquake, and so great.*   Revelation 16: 10, 16-18

Revelation 16:17 reveals that: *It is done*. What is done? We are not told, but we do know that the Tribulation will end at the Battle of Armageddon, and the Battle of Armageddon is the fulfillment of God's plan to defeat Satan, end the Age of Grace (Church Age), save all of Israel who remain alive and launch the 1000 year Millennial Kingdom which will finally allow Israel to settle in the Promised Land.. It has always been God's Plan to redeem His beloved Jews before the 1000-year Millennial Kingdom begins. Redemption to every Jew will be exactly the same as the redemption of every Gentile:

For God so loved the world, that he gave his only begotten Son, that whosoever believeth in him should not perish, but have everlasting life John 3:16

In his letter to the Romans, the Apostle Paul revealed when this would happen.

[25] *For I would not, brethren, that ye should be ignorant of this mystery, lest ye should be wise in your own conceits; that blindness in part is happened to **Israel**, until the **Fulness of the Gentiles** be come in* [26] *And so **all Israel shall be saved**: as it is written, **There shall come out of Sion the Deliverer**, and shall turn away ungodliness from Jacob:* Romans 11: 25-26

The *Fulness of the Gentiles* will come when all that accept Jesus Christ as their Lord and savior will be completed during the current Church Age. In some miraculous way that is not fully explained to us, the *Son of Man will come out of Mt. Zion* and *all Israel shall be saved*. When the Body of Christ is complete (Ephesians 4: 10-16) and all Israel (those who are still alive) are saved…...*IT IS DONE.*

All Christians should live in great expectation of when the Great Tribulation will begin and end. It will start suddenly when the entire world will see a great celestial battle in the heavenlies between Satan and Michael the archangel. It will end at the Battle of Armageddon on the Feast of Yom Kippur. The *Day of the Lord* is without a doubt the Battle of Armageddon, and the *Day of Jesus Christ* is the Rapture of the Saints. We have shown that a 2nd *Day of the Lord* will occur at the end of the Millennial Kingdom. The Christian who studies and understands the Book of Revelation will not be surprised or caught off guard. Watch…wait…and be prepared for the time is near.

[**14**] *Wherefore, beloved, seeing that ye look for such things, be diligent that ye may be found of him in peace, without spot, and blameless.* [**15**] *And account that the longsuffering of our Lord is salvation; even as our beloved brother Paul also according to the wisdom given unto him hath written unto you;* [**16**] *As also in all his epistles, speaking in them of these things; in which are some things hard to be understood, which they that are unlearned*

and unstable wrest, as they do also the other scriptures, unto their own destruction.

[17] Ye therefore, beloved, seeing ye know these things before, beware lest ye also, being led away with the error of the wicked, fall from your own steadfastness.

[18] But grow in grace, and in the knowledge of our Lord and Savior Jesus Christ. To him be glory both now and forever. Amen.
II Peter 3: 14-18

Summary

It has been shown beyond reasonable doubt that a *Pre-tribulation Rapture* is in conflict with the teachings of Jesus Christ (Matthew 24: 1-21 … Particularly Matthew 24: 30-31). The key to determining the when the Rapture and 2nd coming will occur is the *Parable of the Wheat and Tares* and the *Parable of the Sower.*

[3] And he spoke many things unto them in parables, saying, Behold, a sower went forth to sow;

[4] And when he sowed, some seeds fell by the way side, and the fowls came and devoured them up:

[5] Some fell upon stony places, where they had not much earth: and forthwith they sprung up, because they had no deepness of earth:

[6] And when the sun was up, they were scorched; and because they had no root, they withered away.

[7] And some fell among thorns; and the thorns sprung up, and choked them:

[8] But other fell into good ground, and brought forth fruit, some an hundredfold, some sixtyfold, some thirtyfold.

[9] ***Who hath ears to hear, let him hear***   Matthew 13: 3-9

*[18] Hear ye therefore the **Parable of the Sower.***

[19] When any one heareth the word of the kingdom, and understand it not, then cometh the wicked one, and catches away that which was sown in his heart. This is he which received seed by the way side.

[**20**] *But he that received the seed into stony places, the same is he that heareth the word, and anon with joy receives it;*

[**21**] *Yet hath he not root in himself, but he prospers for a while: For when tribulation or persecution arises because of the word, by and by he is offended.*

[**22**] *He also that received seed among the thorns is he that heareth the word; and the care of this world, and the deceitfulness of riches, choke the word, and he becometh unfruitful.*

[**23**] *But he that received seed into the good ground is he that heareth the word, and understands it; which also bears fruit, and bringeth forth, some an hundredfold, some sixty, some thirty.*   Matthew 13: 18-23

[**24**] *Another parable put He forth unto them, saying, The kingdom of heaven is likened unto a man which sowed good seed in his field:*

[**25**] *But while men slept, his enemy came and sowed tares among the wheat, and went his way.*

[**26**] *But when the blade was sprung up, and brought forth fruit, then appeared the tares also.*

[**27**] *So the servants of the householder came and said unto him, Sir, didst not thou sow good seed in thy field? From whence then hath it tares?*

[**28**] *He said unto them: An enemy hath done this. The servants said unto him: Will thou then that we go and gather them up?*

[**29**] *But he said, Nay; lest while ye gather up the tares, ye root up also the wheat with them.*

[**30**] *Let both grow together until the harvest: and in the time of harvest I will say to the reapers,* ***Gather ye together first the tares, and bind them in bundles to burn them: but gather the wheat into my barn***
Matthew 13: 24-30

[**36**] *Then Jesus sent the multitude away, and went into the house: and his disciples came unto him, saying, Declare unto us the parable of the tares of the field.*

[37] *He answered and said unto them, He that soweth the good seed is the Son of man;*

[38] *The field is the world; the good seed are the children of the kingdom; but the tares are the children of the wicked one;*

[39] *The enemy that sowed them is the devil:* **The harvest is the end of the world;** *and the* **reapers are the angels.**

[40] *As therefore the tares are gathered and burned in the fire; so shall it be in the end of this world.*

[41] *The Son of man shall send forth his angels, and they shall gather out of his kingdom all things that offend, and them which do iniquity;*

[42] **And shall cast them into a furnace of fire:** *there shall be wailing and gnashing of teeth.*

[43] *Then shall the righteous shine forth as the sun in the kingdom of their Father.* **Who hath ears to hear, let him hear**

Matthew 13: 36-43

In Matthew 13:30 Jesus said: *Allow both (wheat and tares) to grow together until the harvest; and in the time of the harvest, I will say to the reapers:* **First gather up the tares and bind them in bundles to burn them up; but gather the wheat into my barn** (Matt. 13:30). He then explained that the *tares are sons of the evil one* (Matt. 13:38). This parable does *not* teach that the Rapture and Second Coming will happen together. Although Jesus specifically forbade the removal of the wicked, He *did not* forbid the removal of the righteous (Matt. 13:29). The *Wheat Harvest* is not the *Second Coming* of Christ to earth: It is the *Rapture* of all true believers. The *Burning of the Tares* represents the *Battle of Armageddon* when the Tares will be purged from the earth.

Jesus said unbelievers will be gathered 1st into bundles (groups), but there is no indication that they will immediately be burned (Revelation 19:20). The tares (unbelievers) will not be destroyed until 10 days after the Rapture on the last Jewish *Feast of Yom Kippur* at His 2nd Coming.

[21] *And it shall come to pass in that day, that the LORD shall punish the host of the high ones that are on high, and the kings of the earth upon the earth.*

[22] *And they shall be gathered together, as prisoners are gathered in the pit, and shall be shut up in the prison, and after many days shall they be visited.*

[23] *Then the moon shall be confounded, and the sun ashamed, when the LORD of hosts shall reign in mount Zion, and in Jerusalem, and before his ancients gloriously.*   Isaiah 24: 21-23

The bundling of the tares indicates that following the Rapture, unbelievers will first gather together in fear (Revelation 6:15), and then later they will all be bundled (gathered together) at the Battle of Armageddon (Matthew 24: 29-31, Revelation 14: 15-19). Nothing is strained and everything falls into place.

However, the apostle Paul under the inspiration of the Holy Spirit without ambiguity said the *dead in Christ will rise first* followed by those *believers who are alive.*

[16] *For the Lord himself shall descend from heaven with a shout, with the voice of the archangel, and with the trump of God: and the dead in Christ shall rise first:*

[17] *Then we which are alive and remain shall be caught up together with them in the clouds, to meet the Lord in the air: and so shall we ever be with the Lord*   I Thessalonians 4: 16-17

If the *Rapture* and *Second Coming* both happen together, we have a contradiction in the Bible. However, the mystery is cleared up when we understand that the Rapture of the Church *precedes* the Second Coming by the Jewish *Ten Days of Awe* between Tishri 1 (Feast of Trumpets) and Tishri 10 (Feast of Yom Kippur). The Rapture will occur first, when Christ returns in the clouds to remove His church from earth and take us to heaven. Jesus said: *If I go and prepare a place for you, **I will come again and receive you to Myself**, that where I am (heaven), there you* *may be also*. (John 14:3). Jesus will not touch the earth at the Rapture but will gather all true believers to Him in the heavens.

At this time, the dead in Christ will be resurrected, which is immediately followed by all living Christians being caught up into the clouds to meet Jesus Christ……this is not the 2nd Coming of Jesus Christ. At His Second Coming, Jesus will return to earth and His feet will land on the Mount of Olives; splitting it into two parts (Zechariah 14:4). At that time, He will send out His angels to gather the tares (unbelievers, Revelation 14: 14-20). There will be many Jews who will be saved before the Church Age closes at the Battle of Armageddon, and there will be *Gleanings* which will be harvested during these last 10 days (Leviticus 19:9, Isaiah Chapter 24). The Apostle Paul revealed that at last all of Israel (those still alive) will finally be saved (Romans 11:26). Together, they will inherit the land promised to Abraham, Moses and King David during the 1000-year Millennial Kingdom. Christ will rule as King of Kings and Lord of Lords during these 10000 years with King David by his side. It will be a glorious time and many more will be saved during this 1000-year period. This is the meaning of Revelation 14: 12-1).

During the 10-day of God's Wrath, The *Gleanings* (True believers and new unbelievers) … both grow together. *All* who remain alive will be gathered to Jesus Christ and judged at the *Judgment of the Sheep and Goats*. Those Jews and Gentiles who are gathered and judged for reward in their natural bodies will be joined by those from deep in the Amazon Jungle and other isolated places. All will stay on earth and enter the Millennial kingdom (Zech 14:16)

> Based partly upon *Making Life Count Ministries* P.O. Box 680174 Prattville, Alabama 36068

Maranatha!

(O Lord Come)

Bibliography

Coulter, Fred R., The Appointed Times of Jesus the Messiah, York Publishing Company, PO Box 1038, Hollister, California, 95024-1038

Dake, Finis J., Dake's Annotated Reference Bible, Dake Bible Sales, P.O. Box 1050, Lawrenceville, Ga., 30246

Finegan, Jack, Handbook of Biblical Chronology, Hendrickson Publishing Company, Peabody, Ma.

Good, Joseph, Rosh Hashanah and the Messianic Kingdom to Come, Hatikva Ministries, PO Box 3125, Port Arthur, Texas 77643-0703

Horn H. S. and L. H. Wood, The Chronology of Ezra, TEACH Services, Inc., www.teachservices.com

Larkin, Clarence, Dispensational Truth, P.O. Box 334, Glenside, Pa., 1920

Logos apostolic Church of God and Bible College, Interlinear Greek and Hebrew Translation, Logos apostolic.org, United Kingdom, Logos apostolic.org

Nee, Watchman, Come Lord Jesus, Christian Fellowship Publishers, Inc., 11515 Allecingie Parkway, Richmond, Virginia 23235

Phillips, Don T., The Book of Revelation: *Mysteries Revealed*, 2nd Edition, Virtual Bookworm. com, PO Box 9949, College Station, Tx 77845

Phillips, Don T., The Book of Ruth: *Historical and Prophetic Truths*,

Virtual Bookworm. com, PO Box 9949, College Station, Tx, 77845

Phillips, Don T., Life After Death: *Mysteries Revealed*,
     Virtual Bookworm. com, PO Box 9949, College Station, Tx, 77845

Phillips, Don T., The Eternal Plan of God: *Dispensations, Covenant
     Promises, Salvation*, Virtual Bookworm. com, PO Box 9949, College
     Station, Texas 7784.

Phillips, Don T., *The Birth and Death of Christ*,
     Virtual Bookworm. com, PO Box 9949, College Station, Tx, 77845

Phillips, Don T., The Book of Exodus: *Historical and Prophetic Truths*
     Virtual Bookworm. com, PO Box 9949, College Station, Tx, 77845

Phillips, Don T., A Biblical Chronology from Adam to Christ,
     Virtual Bookworm. com, PO Box 9949, College Station, Tx, 77845

Phillips, Don T., Life After the Great Tribulation: *The Millennial
     Kingdom,* Virtual Bookworm. com, PO Box 9949, College Station,
     Tx, 77845

Phillips, Don T., The Last 50 Days of Jesus Christ
     Virtual Bookworm. com, PO Box 9949, College Station, Tx, 77845

Phillips, Don T., The Daniel 70 Week Prophecy
     Virtual Bookworm. com, PO Box 9949, College Station, Texas
     77845

Phillips, Don T., The Birth of Christ: *A Forensic Analysis*
     Virtual Bookworm. com, PO Box 9949, College Station, Tx,
     77845

Rosenthal, Matthew, The Pre-Wrath Rapture of the Church, Thomas
     Nelson Publishers, Nashville, Tennessee

Ryrie, Charles C., The Ryrie Study Bible, King James Version, Moody
     Press, Chicago. Ill

Salerno, Donald A., Revelation Unsealed, Virtual Bookworm.Com, P.O.
     Box 9949, College Station, Texas, 77842

Thiele, Edwin R., The Mysterious Numbers of the Hebrew Kings:
     Revised Edition, Kregel, Grand Rapids, Michigan

 Thomas, Robert L., Revelation 1-7, An Exegetical Commentary, Moody
     Press, Chicago, Illinois

Thomas, Robert L., Revelation 8-22, An Exegetical Commentary,
     Moody Press, Chicago, Illinois

Van Kampen, Robert, The Sign, Crossway Books, 1300 Crescent Street,
     Wheaton, Illinois 60187

Walvoord, John F., The Millennial Kingdom, Academic Books,
     Zondervan Publishing Company, 1415 Lake Drive S.E., Grand
     Rapids, Michigan 49506

Footnote: This manuscript has drawn upon several excellent
websites found by GOOGLE search. It is my intention to recognize
every biblical scholar and source of   information from those *giants
that walked before me*. This information was sometimes not made
available. In other cases, information was marked open source or not
marked at all. If any author(s) see any material that they want
referenced, please contact me and I will acknowledge their previous
research and scholarly work. In any case, I am extremely grateful for
previous investigations or conclusions that may (or may not) support this
work. God will know them and He will know the source.

Don T. Phillips   Phillipsdon60@gmail.com